GW00778100

Wide Receiver Play
Fundamentals and Techniques

Ron Jenkins, MS

ISBN: 1-58518-652-X
Library of Congress Control Number: 2002104657

Book layout: Jennifer Bokelmann
Cover design: Kerry Hartjen
Front cover photo: Todd Warshaw/Allsport

Coaches Choice
P.O. Box 1828
Monterey, CA 93942
www.coacheschoice.com

DEDICATION

This book is dedicated to the students, administration, staff, and faculty of Bishop Montgomery High School in Torrance, California, and to their principal, Rosemary Libbon, who does brilliant work leading the school.

CONTENTS

INTRODUCTION

Wide receivers in today's modern passing game are one of the cornerstones of any offense. Although recruiting big, fast, and strong wide receivers is the norm today, making receivers successful athletes includes many other attributes. Coaching fundamentally sound mechanics to those who play the position of wide receiver is essential to the increased success of any offense.

This book will give the reader a more thorough understanding of the techniques, mechanics, and thought processes required to play the position of wide receiver at the high school or college level. This book was written for coaches, players, as well as for those parents to help provide athletes with the fundamental skills necessary to play the position of wide receiver efficiently and effectively. Every subject covered is important in the development of the wide receiver at every level of play. Each chapter covers specific wide receiver topics or skills. The reader can go through the book from start to finish to learn what is necessary in playing the position well, or use the book as a reference guide to trouble-shoot areas of concern. Hard work on the mechanics and techniques can measurably develop a wide receiver's consistency.

Although teaching sound mechanics takes time and effort, it is well worth it. When a wide receiver uses good technique and mechanics, he can create better separation from the defender and make the quarterback's job much easier. In addition, with greater space between the receiver and defender comes the increased chance of a substantial run after the catch.

As the various techniques and mechanics are reviewed, there will often be a picture or a drawing to illustrate a point or technique. Hopefully, the written description, along with the picture or illustration, will provide the clarity necessary to teach and learn the skill effectively.

It is my hope that this book will assist coaches and wide receivers in making their offenses more efficient and productive. I think the best way to teach these techniques and skills would be to utilize the *four laws of learning*: explanation (by the coach), demonstration (by the coach or the use of film), imitation (by the player), and many repetitions by the player himself.

My suggestion is that as you learn these techniques, you should start out slowly and build up speed as you master the skills. Start off walking through the techniques, then go to half speed, then full speed. Once you have truly learned the techniques, you will be able to carry them out at full speed during a game with no problem; they will become second nature to you.

Things to Remember as a Wide Receiver

- You should always get to the line of scrimmage quickly. The defense will then give you a pre-snap look that can clue you in on the coverage.

- When you come to the line of scrimmage, you should always check with the sideline referee to make sure you are set properly. They will tell you where you need to be if you line up wrong.

- You should help the quarterback by being aware of possible secondary blitzes from your side of the field. Go ahead and point them out.

- You should always make sure that everyone has been set for at least one count -- before you go in motion. If you notice someone moving, stop your motion for one second, and then continue – or sprint to where you are motioning to -- and then get set just before the ball is snapped.

- You should always practice at full speed! Mentally and physically it trains your mind and body to go full speed during every play in every game.

- You should always run your routes full speed. You should never go half speed and then burst out. It rarely does anything to the defender you are working against, and more often than not, it gives him time to get set for your break.

- You should always accelerate out of your breaks – especially on deep routes. Always accelerate as you look back for the ball.

- If the ball is in the air, it is the receiver's ball. If you can get a hand on the ball, do it, even on crossing routes. Don't duck or pull your arms in because you think a receiver is behind you. If the ball is near you, go get it, or at least get a hand on it.

- When you are running with the ball, and defenders are behind you, run with high knees so that a defender cannot trip you up from behind.

CHAPTER 1

Wide Receiver Fundamentals

The Stance

The wide receiver's feet should be staggered front-to-back and have a comfortable lateral separation to execute an effective start. An effective start means the receiver will roll off of his front foot and bring his back foot through without repositioning his feet, much like a sprinter will in starting blocks. His feet should be staggered far enough apart so that the athlete will not false step (Figure 1-1). A false step is when, at the snap of the ball, the receiver repositions his feet to push off. Usually, the receiver either picks up his front foot and brings it forward, or picks up his back foot and moves it backward. One of the critical elements of effective route running is to close the cushion of the defensive back in a timely fashion, and a false step impedes this intent.

It is the preference of the coach to decide whether the receiver should have his foot closest to the ball up or back. But once the choice has been made, his foot positioning should be consistent. Either the inside foot should always be up no matter what the side the receiver is on, or the inside foot should always be back no matter which side the receiver is on. This is critical to get the routes to *time-out* consistently with the quarterback's throw.

Figure 1-1. This is a good, solid stance.

- This receiver has elected to keep has hands at chest level – which has become vogue in recent years.

- The receiver's feet are staggered far enough apart so that he won't false step when he releases downfield.

You should have the receiver's outside foot back because most of the releases versus bump-and-run defenders are outside releases (Figure 1-2). The reasons for this are simple.

Figure 1-2.

- In this case, the receiver should have his hands at chest level so he can slap the defender's hands away should he attempt to jam him.

- Against a bump-and-run defender, the receiver will bring his feet closer together because his first step will be lateral, rather than forward (See Chapter 6 detailing bump-and-run defenders).

When a receiver takes an inside release versus a bump-and-run defender, the defender will jump to the inside of the receiver's hip because he knows the receiver is taking the inside release to run an inside breaking route. In addition, when the receiver takes an inside release, the defender can peek in the backfield and see what kind of drop the quarterback is taking, which would really hurt the pattern if it was a quick, three-step drop.

When the receiver takes an outside release, he can break anywhere he wants to, depending on the type of release he wants to use (speed, one-step, or double-step). The defender will then have his back to the quarterback as well as the rest of the field. He is totally focused on the receiver he is attempting to cover. The receiver can then manipulate what the defender does by using the various techniques that will be covered in this book.

Body-Lean and Run Technique

The wide receiver needs a good body lean to be able to accelerate, cut, and break down in a concise area. Usually a receiver will start to pop up when attempting to do anything other than run a straight line. The defender is coached to recognize a deviation in body lean and is alerted that the receiver is about to make a move. Usually a 55- to 75-degree body lean is adequate in most pass routes, and should be maintained throughout the route (Figure 1-3).

Figure 1-3. This receiver demonstrates excellent body lean and arm movement.

- The receiver is looking downfield.

- His arms are at 90-degree angles.

- He has excellent body-lean.

- His knees are coming up high.

The receiver also has to pay attention to his arm movements. He should always concentrate on arm movement that simulates the movements used when running. Some receivers will drop their arms, stick their arms out, or even raise their arms up in the air when they start to breakdown. This is an obvious signal that a receiver is about to make a move, and tips off the defender, allowing him to prepare for it.

Vertical Push

Vertical push is one of the most important tools for today's wide receiver. Vertical push is the ability to get downfield as quickly as possible to create problems for the defensive secondary. Remember, the further you get downfield, the fewer the number of defenders available to cover the whole field. In addition, by getting vertical push as quickly as possible, you force the defender to make reactionary adjustments.

Of course, it helps if receivers have great speed, but the principals of vertical push can be utilized by individual receivers if they understand that they have to do the best they can to get downfield as fast as they can. Hesitation moves and counter routes don't really do anything unless the receiver (and the offense) runs full speed during every single given play.

Creating Separation

Creating separation refers to the receiver's ability to break away from a defender just as the football is being thrown to him. The receiver should be catching the ball in *space* to create yardage after the catch.

Creating separation requires the receiver first know how to set up and generate a situation where he can get maximum separation at an advantageous point in the route. The receiver must then be in complete control of his body and how he runs the pass route. To do this takes hours of refinement and proper instruction. The receiver must *react* on the football field and do the thinking in practice. Most importantly, creating great separation requires that the receiver get into, and out of, his breaks cleanly and efficiently.

Catching the Football

Catching the football is one of the most important aspects of being a wide receiver. Your receivers could be the fastest player on the team and run the best routes, and also have the innate ability to create a big play after the catch with a great run, but if they don't catch the football, the play is wasted, and the clock stops--period. The following are 10 simple rules your receivers should know when catching the football (these rules will be expanded on in the remainder of this chapter):

- The receiver should reach out to catch the pass (he shouldn't try to catch it against his body).
- The receiver should watch the ball into his hands.
- The receiver should catch the football with his fingertips.
- The receiver should catch the football with his *palms up* when running away from the quarterback (unless the ball is thrown behind him — then he should come back and get it at its highest point with his *palms out* — See Figure 1-4).
- When catching a pass in stride, the receiver should always wait until the last second before reaching out for the football.
- The receiver should catch the football with his *palms out* when running towards the quarterback (except if the ball is at his stomach level or below).
- The receiver should use his body as a shield when going up for the ball in traffic.
- The receiver should catch the pass first, and then make the run.
- When the ball is in the air, the receiver should go get it. Rather than waiting for it, he should come back to the football whenever possible.
- The receiver should catch the ball with two hands; it is rare that receivers make one-handed catches consistently.

The ability to catch the football is predominantly mental, which means that anyone can become a better pass catcher with the proper technique, lots of repetitions, and the ability to focus on the football when the ball is in the air. This is accomplished in team practice sessions and lots of individual work.

The most important thing to be aware of is that the ability to make all the catches in game situations starts with thinking about and planning how to catch each given pass in practice. The receivers should be getting lots of repetitions catching the ball the proper way. This will produce muscle memory making those catches in game situations automatic. If the receiver has to think about how to catch a given pass when it's happening in a game, the chances of catching that pass decrease dramatically.

It's vital for a receiver to catch the football away from his body, so he can see the football make contact with his hands. When a receiver lets the football hit his body, he has less control over the catch and the football can easily bounce off his body, or slip through his arms.

It is also important for him to come back to the football whenever possible (Figure 1-4). This creates immediate separation from the defender, if he doesn't already have it.

Figure 1-4.

• The receiver is reaching out for the football and catching it with palms out. He is also coming back to the football.

When you tell your receivers to *catch the football with your hands*, you are actually telling them to *catch the football with your fingertips*. This allows a certain amount of give that keeps the ball from bouncing off the palm of their hands (Figure 1-5).

Figure 1-5.

• The catch is made with the fingertips, which allows the *give* necessary to prevent the ball from bouncing off the palms of the hand.

When a receiver is running a route away from the quarterback (corner routes, streaks, and posts), he should have his hands open so his palms are facing the sky. The reason for this is because as he runs away from the quarterback, he wants to keep his momentum going in the same direction of the football. Placing his hands any other way forces him to turn his body and reduces his speed. In addition, having you're his hands *palms up* increases his reach (Figure 1-6).

Figure 1-6.

- The receiver is running his route away from the quarterback, and catching the pass with his *palms up*. Catching the ball with his *palms up* increases his reach.

- He is also watching the football all the way into his hands.

However, if the receiver is running a streak or deep-post route downfield and the ball is thrown behind him with defenders in the area, he must catch the ball at its highest point. He does this by turning his body towards the quarterback, opening his palms to the football, and assertively making the catch. This will obviously slow him down, but is necessary given the circumstances of this situation (Figure 1-7).

Figure 1-7.

- The receiver is running a deep route, but the ball was thrown behind him.

- The receiver must then come back to the football and catch it at its highest point with his *palms out*.

When catching any pass, especially passes where the receiver is running full speed downfield, it is critical that he doesn't reach for the ball too early. This will slow him down considerably, and will throw off his balance. It is impossible for a receiver to run at top speed with his arms stretched out for the pass. He must wait until the last second before reaching for the football (Figure 1-8).

Figure 1-8.

- The receiver is running a deep route. It's very important that he wait until the last possible second to reach out and catch the football. This allows him to keep his speed and run through the football.

- Catching the ball with *palms up* increases his reach.

- Putting his hands out too soon will slow him down considerably.

When the receiver runs a curl route, or any route when he is back coming towards the quarterback, he should reach for the pass with his hands *palms out* (except when the pass is going to be caught at or below the stomach level). He should reach out for the football and catch it with his hands. Many times, if it hits his body, it can bounce off of his pads because he can't watch the ball make contact with his body, and his pads don't have any give (Figures 1-9 through 1-11).

Sometimes the receiver has to catch the ball in traffic. Maybe he's running a crossing route over the middle of the field and one (or both) of the safeties is coming up to make the play. In this case he should use his body to act as a barrier between the football and the defender. Then he will reach out and make the catch away from his body, and prevent the defender from getting his hands on or near the football (Figure 1-12).

Many times the receiver will be in a hurry to make a play and start running before he makes the catch and secures the football, resulting in a dropped pass. It is critical that he makes the catch first before trying to run with the football. This requires discipline in practice, so it becomes automatic during games. He must make the catch first before making any attempt to run downfield with the football.

Figure 1-9.	**Figure 1-10.**	**Figure 1-11.**

The receiver is running a curl route. He has his palms out because the ball is above his mid-section.	The receiver is running a route across the middle of the field. Since the ball is above his mid-section, he should catch the pass with his palms out.	This receiver is running a curl route. The ball is thrown below his mid-section and he should catch the ball with his palms up.

Figure 1-12.

- The receiver is using his body here to shield the defender from the football. The defender will not be able to get to the football.

Keep in mind that any ball in the air is intended for an offensive receiver. In other words, if the ball is in the air, your receiver should go get it! He should come back to the football whenever possible. Too many times the ball is in the air and the receiver decides to wait for it to come to him, rather that going after the football. The defender then has an opportunity to either knock down the pass before it gets to the receiver, or worse -- the defender has an opportunity to make an interception. Receivers should always try to make the catch, and never allow the defender to intercept the pass.

The receiver might look back for the pass, and automatically think he can't get to the football, so he gives up on the ball right away. This is one of the worst things a receiver can do. The fact is, many times the receiver is wrong in his assessment, and can actually get to the football. All receivers should run through all passes. If a receiver accelerates to the football every time he looks back for the pass, he will get to many of the balls he thought he could not get to. This acceleration will also help the receiver separate from the defender, which will allow the receiver room to make the catch.

Finally, the receiver should always attempt to make the catch with both hands. It is rare that receivers make one-handed catches. It does happen, but if he can't do it consistently in practice, the chances of doing it in a game are poor. He should always make catches with both hands. This is a habit that should be engrained in muscle-memory during practices, and will then transfer to game situations.

CHAPTER 2

Pass-Route Releases

The term *release* refers to the initial part of the route within five yards of the line of scrimmage. It also has to do with what the receiver is doing at the beginning of his route with respect to the defense and/or a specific defender. Releases can do several things that may include: moving a defender, getting to a specific area of the field at a specific time, changing up the initial look of the route from the defenders point of view, or closing the initial cushion of the defender putting him in a vulnerable position.

The Vertical Release

This is an excellent release, especially if you have superior talent. The defenders have to come to the receivers if the receivers are athletically superior to the defender. The reason for this is that because of the receiver's speed, the defender has to do his best to be close the receiver when the ball is in the air. The only way that the defender can really cover the receiver's route is to guess where the receiver is trying to go, and then impede his path. If they guess wrong, the receiver will be wide open (Figure 2-1).

Figure 2-1.

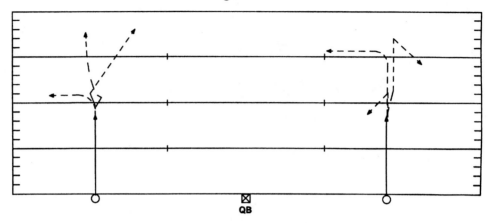

The Attack Release

This release attacks the defender's leverage in relation to the receiver. The receiver will run directly at the defender to get him squared-up. It is imperative that the receiver runs directly at the defender. This means that the receiver centers his body directly in front of the defender with no deviation to one side or the other. This is very hard to perfect and can take several weeks of practice. Usually a receiver will unconsciously pick a side of the defender to attack. Attacking a shoulder allows the defender to open his hips to the side that the receiver is attacking (Figure 2-2).

Attacking one side or the other can present two problems. First, if the receiver is running a route to the side of the defender he is attacking, the defender can get a jump in coverage by being able to open his hips early and be able to comfortably *jump the route*. Second, if the receiver attacks the opposite side of the defender, the receiver has to cross the defender's body to run the route. If the receiver is too close to the defender when attempting to cross his face, the defender can step in front of him and cut off the receiver's route. If the receiver crosses the defender's face too early in the route, this slows the development of the route and allows the defender to maintain his cushion and give him an advantage in coverage.

A major advantage to the attack release is that it allows the receiver to break the defender's cushion because the defender cannot quickly gain depth backpedaling. This puts the defender in a vulnerable position because the receiver can run anywhere he wants to and the defender has no advantage in leverage.

One of the exceptions to this release would be when the receiver wanted to run either a quick seven-yard out, or a deeper 12-yard out, versus a defender who is using an inside-leverage technique. In both of these cases, the rule is to *leave the defender inside, and use a vertical release.*

Figure 2-2.

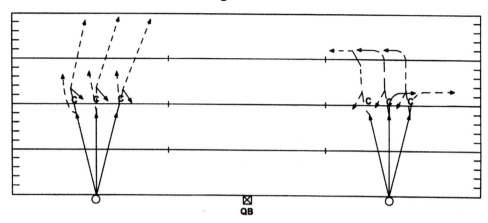

Seam and Burst Releases

Receivers use different seam and burst releases for two primary reasons. One, the receiver may want to *move* the defensive back inside or outside in relation to his starting point. Two, the receiver may want to get to a particular of the field before making his final break.

Versus a cornerback who is playing man-off coverage, the receiver can use a seam release to cause the defender to slide inside initially. Then, when the receiver snaps his hips to a vertical position and accelerates upfield, the defender will have a tendency to turn his shoulders upfield, allowing the receiver to make a break away from him to gain greater separation. Against a zone defense, the same seam release will enable the receiver to get to the middle of the field more quickly to find a more advantageous passing lane to receive the pass.

Defining Snap

Snap refers to the receiver's ability to change his direction in a sharp and distinctive manor by placing his lead foot at almost a 45-degree angle, and then snapping his hips at the same time to head vertically downfield.

On the snap of the ball, the receiver will head downfield at about a 60-degree angle. As the receiver hits his fourth step on his *seam release* (the fifth step on his *burst release*), he will plant his lead foot parallel with the sideline, and accelerate vertically (Figures 2-3 and 2-4). The break should be distinct, yet executed in a smooth manor. The deviation laterally should be between two and two and a half yards maximum, and the receiver should be close to four- or five-yards downfield when he snaps vertically. This takes time and effort, but will greatly enhance the receiver's repertoire of tools as far as his routes are concerned.

Figure 2-3.

- This receiver is just hitting his fourth step in his seam (inside) release.

- When first learning the snap technique, receivers can watch their step here to make sure they place it parallel with the sideline.

- However, when running routes against a defense, the receiver should *never* look at the ground.

Figure 2-4.

- This receiver is just hitting his fifth step in his burst (outside) release.

- The receiver does a good job of placing his lead foot so that it is parallel with the sideline when he snaps his route.

- His hips are pointed vertically downfield.

The Seam Release

This release is most often used when the receiver lines up wider than normal, or a normal split, relative to the spot of the ball. This type of release can be used to get across the middle faster, or to trick the corner into giving you to one of the safeties (as in a zone defense) regardless of what he is trained to do. This is a great release to use against man or zone defenders (Figure 2-5).

Figure 2-5.

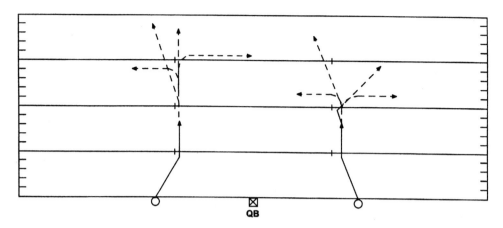

The angle of the seam release is at about 60 degrees, because you want the receiver to threaten the corner deep. He must really *snap* his hips when he breaks vertically for the release to do the most damage to the defender's leverage.

On the snap of the ball, the receiver will pick up his front foot and place it in the direction of the seam release (this does not count as a step). Then the receiver will *snap* his route into the vertical stem of the route on his fourth step.

The Burst Release

This release is most often used when the receiver lines up in a tighter than normal position, to give a pre-snap look to the defense, but then releases outward once the ball is snapped before transitioning to a vertical stem. Many times receivers will be running some kind of route over the middle of the field such as a dig, square-in route, or a post (Figure 2-6).

Figure 2-6.

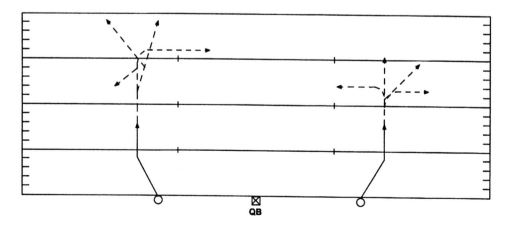

The angle of the burst release is at about 60 degrees. You don't want the receiver running so flat that he is not making ground upfield. The receiver is moving downfield more that he is widening to the sideling. He must *snap* his hips when he breaks vertically for the release to have the full effect, and must always use a vertical stem after the burst before making the final break in his route. The point that he *snaps* into the vertical stem should be exactly at the position he would line up in if he were to run the route using a vertical stem. The receiver will *snap* his route into his vertical stem on the fifth step from the line of scrimmage.

CHAPTER 3

Breaks and Separation

The ability to make precise breaks in a route and separate from the defender is what makes a great receiver. The receiver must concentrate on keeping his body lean and not giving the defender any clue as to which direction he will break to, and then accelerate out of the break creating great separation. Three basic types of breaks used by receivers are the speed cut, the comeback cut, and the breakdown cut.

As the receiver comes off the line of scrimmage, he should get his speed up to nearly full speed – yet controlled. It is important that the receiver not slow down before going into his cut.

The Speed Cut

Three critical steps to the speed cut with correlating body movements are as follows:

- The receiver starts to break down with his foot that is on the outside of the break; that is, if the receiver is breaking to his left, he will start to break with his right foot. This step is called a *pressure step* and is executed at a 45-degree angle. At the same time the receiver should snap his head back to the quarterback to find the football (Figure 3-1).

- As the receiver leans into the route, he needs to take his second step and put it perpendicular to the sideline.

- His third step should be an acceleration step coming out of the cut.

It is important that the receiver be very smooth throughout the route, and accelerates out of the cut. This takes many hours of practice, but once perfected, is near impossible to defend in zone or man coverages.

Figure 3-1. The receiver is breaking to his left in the speed cut.

• This type of cut is used on routes breaking to the outside that are usually no deeper than 12 yards, as well as routes that break over the middle of the field. The speed cut can also be used when a receiver goes in motion and breaks upfield at the snap of the ball.

• The receiver is snapping his head back to find the ball the instant he plants his pressure step.

• He will throw his left elbow back at the same time he snaps his head.

• The *pressure step* is applied at a 45-degree angle.

The Comeback Cut

This type of break is used on curl routes and comeback routes. Although this is a simple route to run, many times the technique of the receiver can be enhanced to be more effective. Two critical steps for the comeback cut are as follows:

1) The *four-step breakdown technique*

2) A *pressure step* that promotes separation from the defender

In approaching the *four-step breakdown*, the receiver is running at near full speed. He starts to break down with the foot that is on the inside of the break; that is, if the receiver is coming back to his left, he will start to break down with his left foot.

Most receivers break down with the outside foot, but breaking down with the inside foot helps the receiver in two ways. First, breaking down to a complete stop while running at near full speed only takes four steps, not five. Second, by breaking down with the inside foot, the receiver keeps his shoulders square upfield, and keeps the defender at bay, not knowing which way the receiver is about to break.

As the receiver starts out of his break with the *pressure step* at a 45-degree angle, he should already have his head snapped back to the quarterback as he pushes off back towards the football (Figure 3-2). This coming back towards the ball is extremely important because it creates a separation from the defender. On occasion, the cornerback may have the receiver covered up to this point, but the receiver can create separation from the cornerback by coming back to the ball to finish the route off and make the catch.

Figure 3-2.

- The receiver does a great job of snapping his head back to the ball just as he hits his pressure- step.

- He has great body lean, and his arms are in a *runner's* position.

- This is an excellent example of applying the pressure-step.

This created separation will also allow the receiver the opportunity to gain yardage after the reception. The yardage gained after any catch is vitally important to the success of the offense and the football team.

The Breakdown Cut

This is a simple break used primarily by the inside receivers on routes that break at 90-degree angles. This cut is very similar to the comeback cut in that is begins with the four-step breakdown technique. However, instead of directly coming back to the ball, the receiver breaks at 90 degrees either in or out. Two critical steps for the breakdown cut are as follows:

- The receiver starts to break down with the foot that is on the inside of the break; that is, if the receiver is breaking to his left, he will start the break with his left foot. This step is called a *breakdown-step*.

- He should snap his head back to the quarterback at the same time the *pressure step* is applied.

The receiver comes off the ball at near full speed. He runs downfield being cognizant of where he wants to go and where the open area is going to be. The defensive back's main focus is on the wide receiver area and so any moves the receiver uses has little or no effect on the defender. The receiver can make his cut directly out of his break, or use a single or double-step move to beat the defender (Figure 3-3). At the defined breaking point, he should plant his *pressure step* at a 45-degree angle, and at the same time snap his head back to find the football, accelerating out of the break away from the defender.

Figure 3-3.

- The receiver is looking directly at the defender.

- His shoulders are over his feet as he breaks down.

- His arms are in close to his body and still maintaining a running posture.

- He is in the second step of his four-step breakdown.

- As he hits his last step, he will snap his head back to find the football, and break laterally.

The primary reason this technique works is that the receiver is separating from the defensive back very quickly into the open area. The receiver can also lean into his defender and prevent him from jumping the route.

All of the techniques discussed should be practiced regularly. Filming the receiver's routes would be an asset, and would speed the learning process. Each receiver will run the routes in his own way, but the overall technique will be the same for all receivers. The best and fastest way to learn proper route technique is to have your receivers watch an experienced, successful receiver, and then have them emulate his body movements.

CHAPTER 4

Individual Pass Routes
Versus Various Coverages

Figure 4-1.

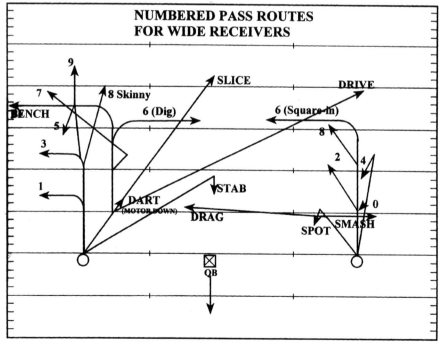

The odd numbered routes go to the outside.   The even numbered routes go to the inside.
Always remember – the larger the number, the deeper the route.

Figure 4-2.

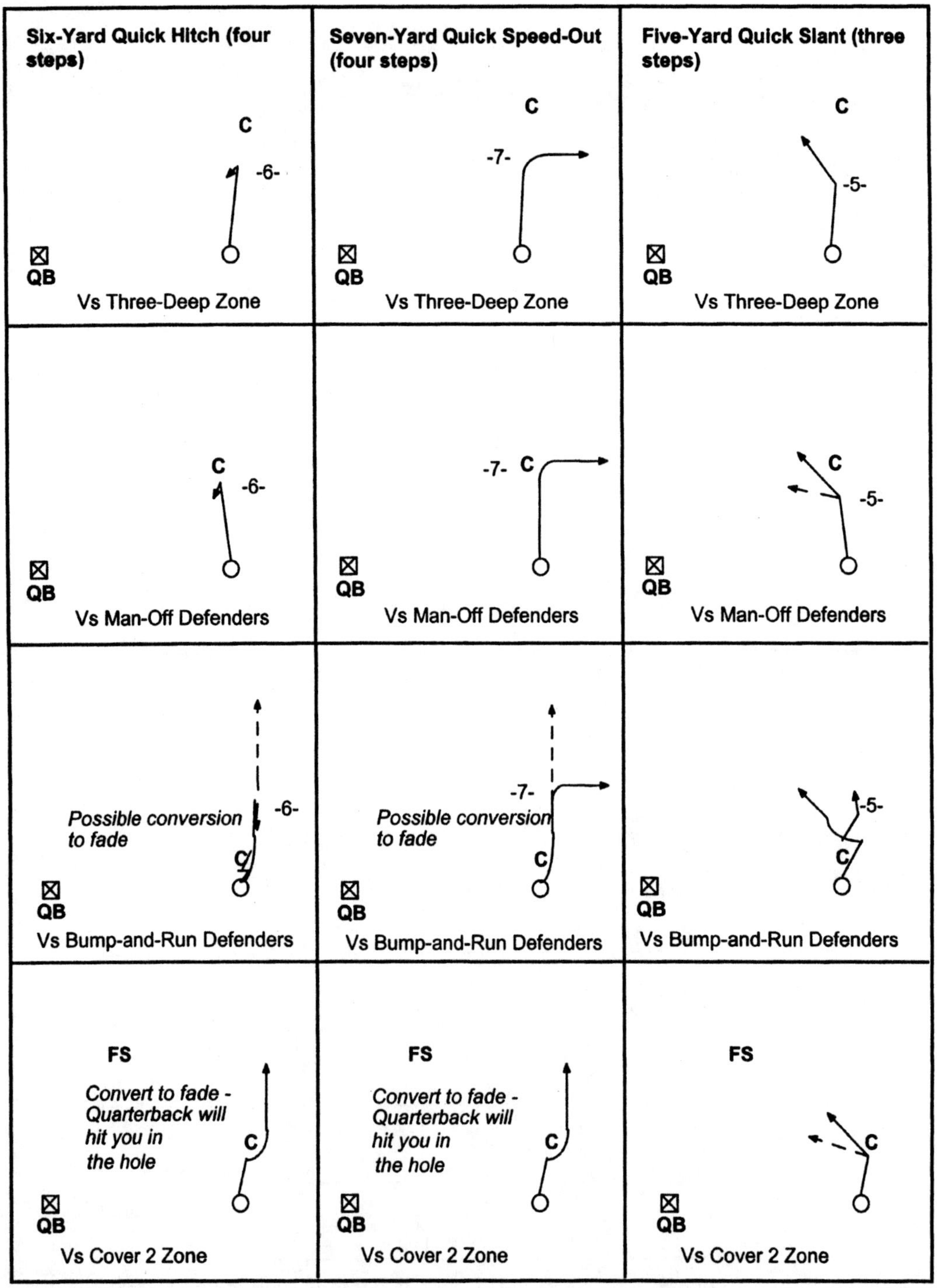

Six-Yard Quick Hitch (four steps)	Seven-Yard Quick Speed-Out (four steps)	Five-Yard Quick Slant (three steps)
C -6- ☒ QB ○ Vs Three-Deep Zone	C -7- ☒ QB ○ Vs Three-Deep Zone	C -5- ☒ QB ○ Vs Three-Deep Zone
C -6- ☒ QB ○ Vs Man-Off Defenders	-7- C ☒ QB ○ Vs Man-Off Defenders	C -5- ☒ QB ○ Vs Man-Off Defenders
Possible conversion to fade -6- ☒ QB C ○ Vs Bump-and-Run Defenders	Possible conversion to fade -7- ☒ QB C ○ Vs Bump-and-Run Defenders	-5- ☒ QB C ○ Vs Bump-and-Run Defenders
FS Convert to fade - Quarterback will hit you in the hole C ☒ QB ○ Vs Cover 2 Zone	FS Convert to fade - Quarterback will hit you in the hole C ☒ QB ○ Vs Cover 2 Zone	FS C ☒ QB ○ Vs Cover 2 Zone

Figure 4-3.

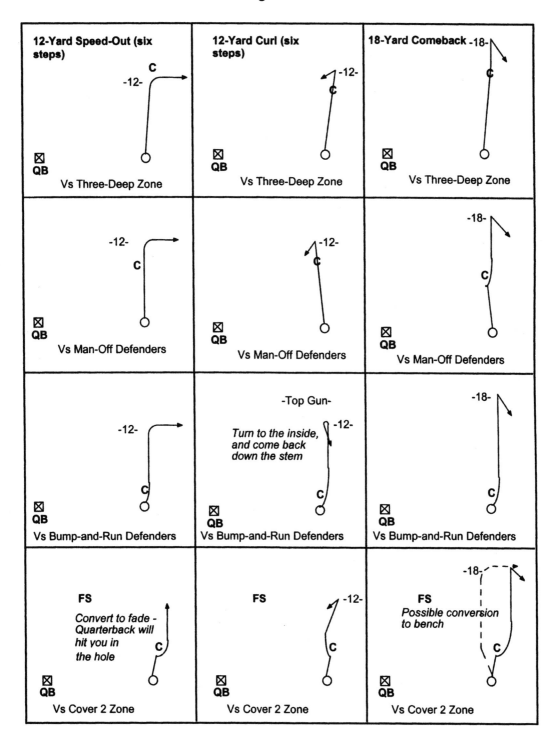

12-Yard Speed-Out (six steps)	12-Yard Curl (six steps)	18-Yard Comeback
Vs Three-Deep Zone	Vs Three-Deep Zone	Vs Three-Deep Zone
Vs Man-Off Defenders	Vs Man-Off Defenders	Vs Man-Off Defenders
Vs Bump-and-Run Defenders	-Top Gun- *Turn to the inside, and come back down the stem* Vs Bump-and-Run Defenders	Vs Bump-and-Run Defenders
FS *Convert to fade - Quarterback will hit you in the hole* Vs Cover 2 Zone	FS Vs Cover 2 Zone	FS *Possible conversion to bench* Vs Cover 2 Zone

Figure 4-4.

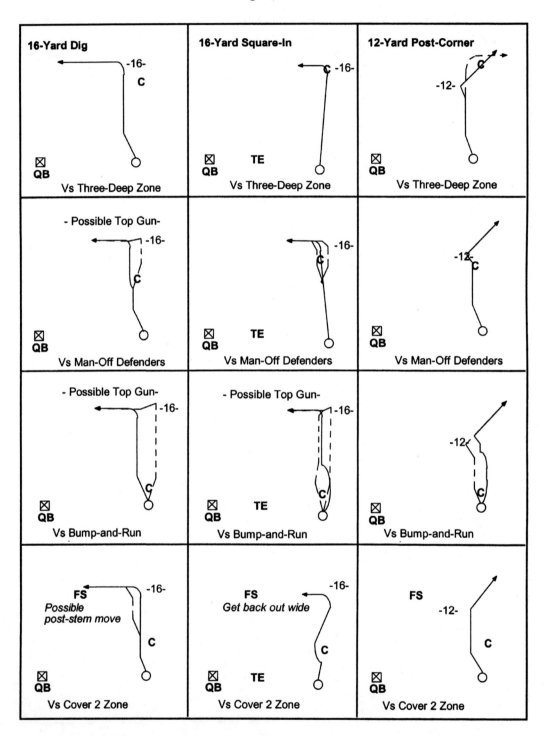

16-Yard Dig — -16- C — QB — Vs Three-Deep Zone

16-Yard Square-In — C -16- — QB — TE — Vs Three-Deep Zone

12-Yard Post-Corner — C -12- — QB — Vs Three-Deep Zone

- Possible Top Gun- — -16- C — QB — Vs Man-Off Defenders

-16- C — QB — TE — Vs Man-Off Defenders

-12- C — QB — Vs Man-Off Defenders

- Possible Top Gun- -16- C — QB — Vs Bump-and-Run

- Possible Top Gun- -16- C — QB — TE — Vs Bump-and-Run

-12- C — QB — Vs Bump-and-Run

FS — Possible post-stem move — -16- C — QB — Vs Cover 2 Zone

FS — Get back out wide — -16- C — QB — TE — Vs Cover 2 Zone

FS — -12- C — QB — Vs Cover 2 Zone

Figure 4-5.

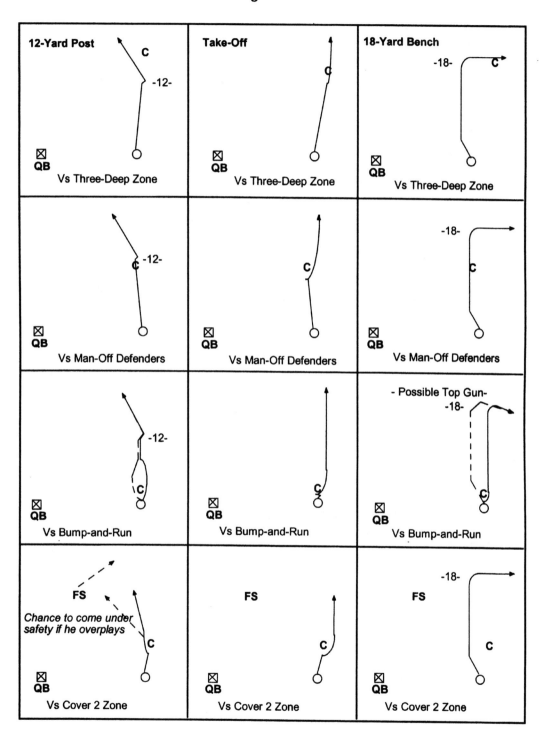

12-Yard Post	**Take-Off**	**18-Yard Bench**
Vs Three-Deep Zone	Vs Three-Deep Zone	Vs Three-Deep Zone
Vs Man-Off Defenders	Vs Man-Off Defenders	Vs Man-Off Defenders
Vs Bump-and-Run	Vs Bump-and-Run	- Possible Top Gun - / Vs Bump-and-Run
Chance to come under safety if he overplays / Vs Cover 2 Zone	Vs Cover 2 Zone	Vs Cover 2 Zone

Figure 4-6.

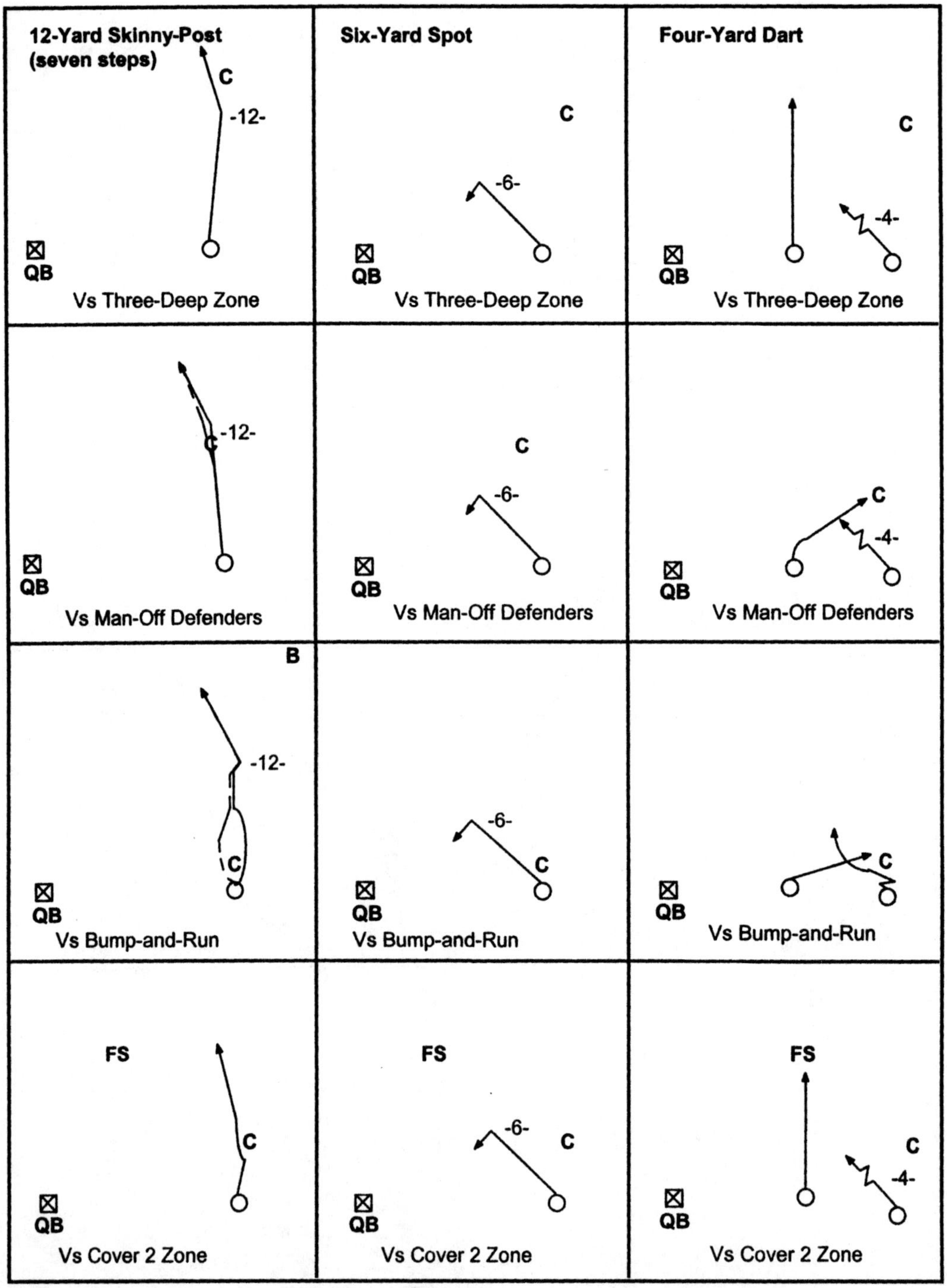

12-Yard Skinny-Post (seven steps)	Six-Yard Spot	Four-Yard Dart
Vs Three-Deep Zone	Vs Three-Deep Zone	Vs Three-Deep Zone
Vs Man-Off Defenders	Vs Man-Off Defenders	Vs Man-Off Defenders
Vs Bump-and-Run	Vs Bump-and-Run	Vs Bump-and-Run
Vs Cover 2 Zone	Vs Cover 2 Zone	Vs Cover 2 Zone

Figure 4-7.

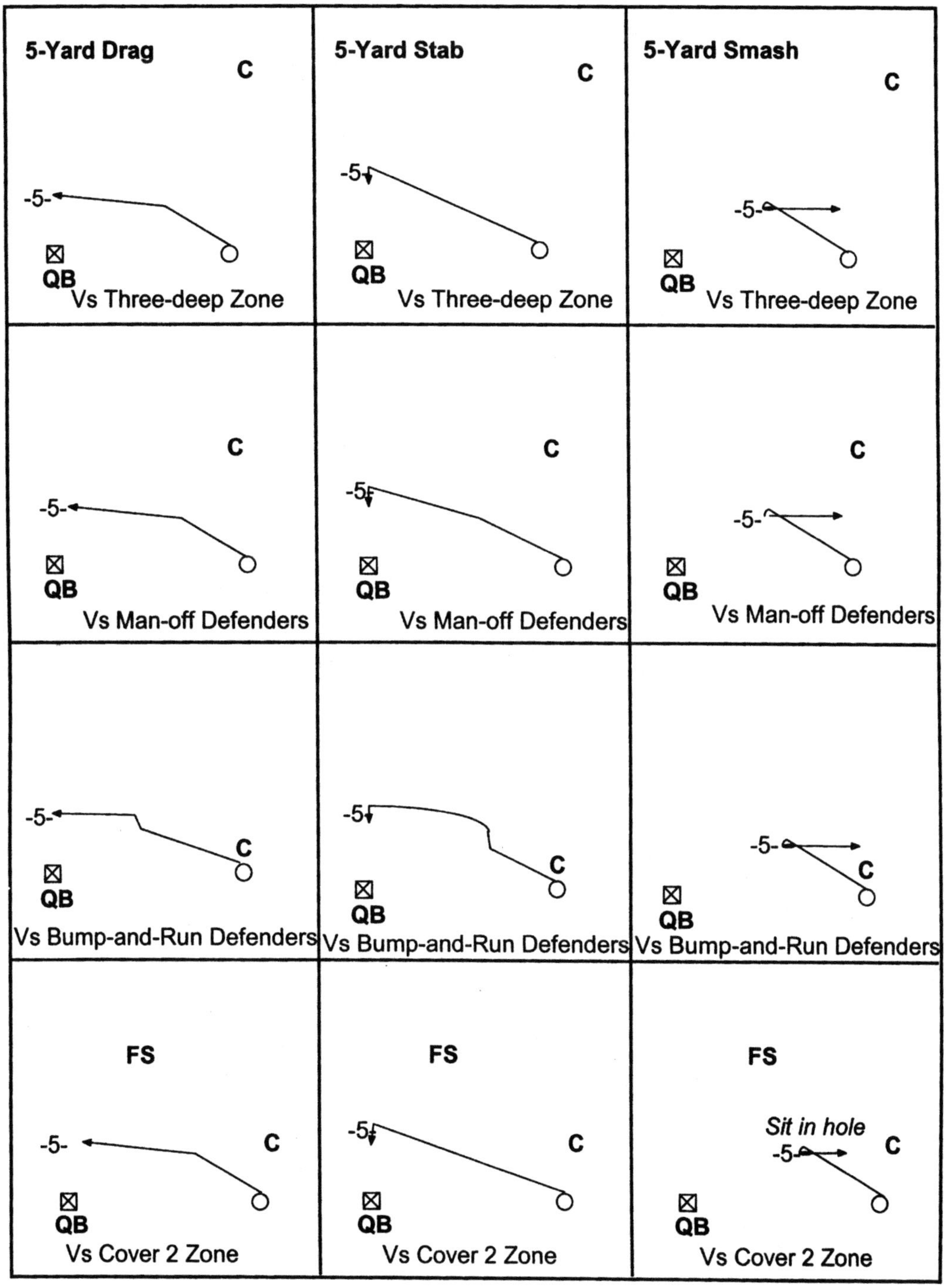

5-Yard Drag — C — -5- — QB — Vs Three-deep Zone
5-Yard Stab — C — -5 — QB — Vs Three-deep Zone
5-Yard Smash — C — -5- — QB — Vs Three-deep Zone

C — -5- — QB — Vs Man-off Defenders
C — -5 — QB — Vs Man-off Defenders
C — -5- — QB — Vs Man-off Defenders

-5- — C — QB — Vs Bump-and-Run Defenders
-5 — C — QB — Vs Bump-and-Run Defenders
-5- — C — QB — Vs Bump-and-Run Defenders

FS — -5- — C — QB — Vs Cover 2 Zone
FS — -5 — C — QB — Vs Cover 2 Zone
FS — Sit in hole — -5- — C — QB — Vs Cover 2 Zone

Figure 4-8.

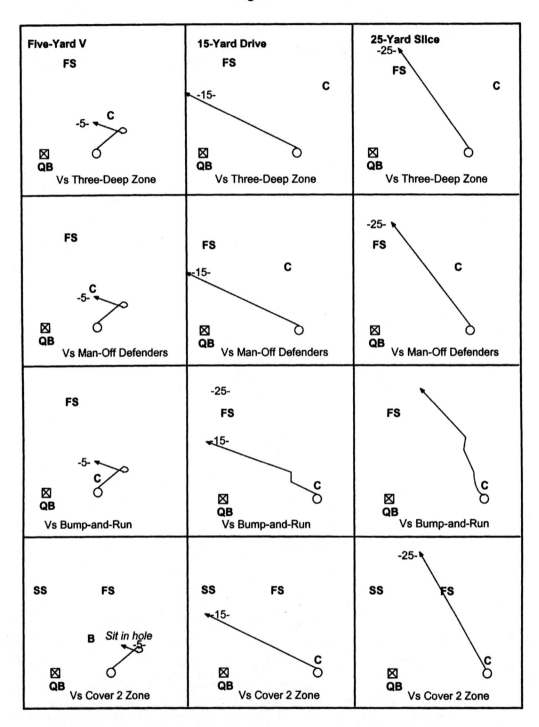

Five-Yard V	15-Yard Drive	25-Yard Slice
Vs Three-Deep Zone	Vs Three-Deep Zone	Vs Three-Deep Zone
Vs Man-Off Defenders	Vs Man-Off Defenders	Vs Man-Off Defenders
Vs Bump-and-Run	Vs Bump-and-Run	Vs Bump-and-Run
Vs Cover 2 Zone	Vs Cover 2 Zone	Vs Cover 2 Zone

CHAPTER 5

Base Pass Routes and Techniques

Three-Deep Zone Routes

Cover 3 zone is a fundamentally sound defense. However, as long as the offense is patient, it should be able to *nickel and dime* its way down the field. Many areas on the field can be attacked provided the receivers run disciplined routes and the quarterback knows where to go with the football.

The second-level coverage (the linebackers) has only four defenders available to cover the field horizontally. This means that there are certain areas on the field an offense can take advantage of. Curl routes, dig routes, sideline routes, and double square-in patterns are all appropriate to call versus this type of coverage. Although it is somewhat unlikely that an offense can throw deep attacking from a standard offensive set, a four- receiver set with all four receivers running go routes with good spacing can create an immediate big play.

Three-deep zone coverage is probably the easiest coverage for the wide receiver to be successful against. The coverage is designed to prevent the big play and to allow the offensive passing game to methodically move downfield.

The basic three-deep zone defense has four defenders dropping to a depth of 12 yards with three defenders covering the deep areas of the field. The remaining four defenders are rushing the quarterback. The defensive back's first priority is the pass. The general rule is to make sure that the defensive backs don't get beat deep (Figure 5-1).

Figure 5-1.

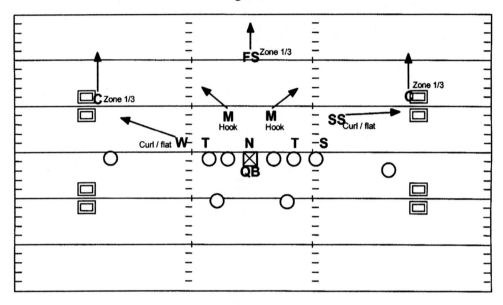

STRENGTHS

1. Three-deep secondary
2. Four-man rush
3. Run support to strong safety

WEAKNESSES

1. Weakside curl/flat
2. Strongside curl
3. Limited fronts
4. Flood routes
5. Run support away from SS
6. Dig routes (square-in route)
7. Four verticals

The corners usually play about 8 to 10 yards off the receiver and slightly to the outside so they can watch the quarterback's drop. The free safety is usually at about 12-yards off the line of scrimmage and in the middle of the field, or even the middle of the offensive formation. The strong safety and the weakside outside linebacker have primarily the same assignments as far as the passing game is concerned: curl to flat on the outside. The remaining two linebackers have the inside-hook areas. The receiver's primary goal is to find the holes in the defense, make the catch, and then make yardage after the reception.

Quick Hitch

Figure 5-2.Route: Zero versus the three-deep zone.

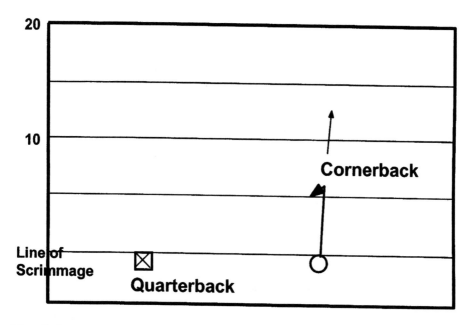

Coaching Points:

- The receiver should burst off the line of scrimmage and run downfield attacking the defender.
- The receiver should begin his breakdown on the fourth (inside foot) step and pivot on the fifth *pressure step*.
- As the receiver snaps his head back to find the quarterback, he should be a stationary target as he finds the ball.He shouldn't drift from the ball.
- After securing the ball, the receiver should take a jab step inside and break to the outside (usually).
  - √ Check the game plan – He can either stay with the route versus press (recommended), or convert the route to a fade.
  - √ He should convert the route to a fade versus cover 2, or a rolled-up corner.

Note: This is a good route to call when the defender is off, and should be good for at least six yards. This can also set up the hitch pump. The hitch pump is called when the defender is likely to come up fast when he reads a three-step drop, and attack the inside of the receiver.

Quick Speed Out

Figure 5-3. Route: 1 versus the three-deep zone.

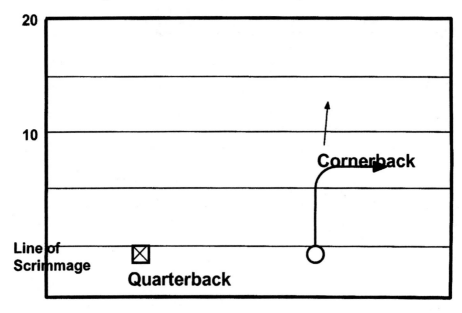

Coaching Points:

- The receiver should burst off the line of scrimmage and run downfield.
  - √ If the defender is inside, the receiver should leave him inside and run a vertical stem.
  - √ If he as head-up or outside, the receiver should attack him.
- The receiver should make eye contact at a spot right between the defender's eyes.
- On fourth step, the receiver should break to the sideline using the *pressure step* (inside foot) to then start his *speed cut.*
- As the receiver snaps his head back to find the quarterback, he should be accelerating out of his break.
- Once the receiver catches the ball, he should break vertically upfield.
  - √ Check the game plan – He can either stay with the route versus press (recommended), or convert the route to a fade.
  - √ He should convert the route to a fade versus cover 2, or a rolled-up corner.

Note: This is a good route to call when the defender is way off, or when you want to stop the clock by stepping out of bounds. *If* the defender comes up hard on this route, a pump would be an appropriate call. However, if the defender plays off, a pump will do little to get the receiver deep downfield.

Quick Slant

Figure 5-4. Route: 2 versus the three-deep zone.

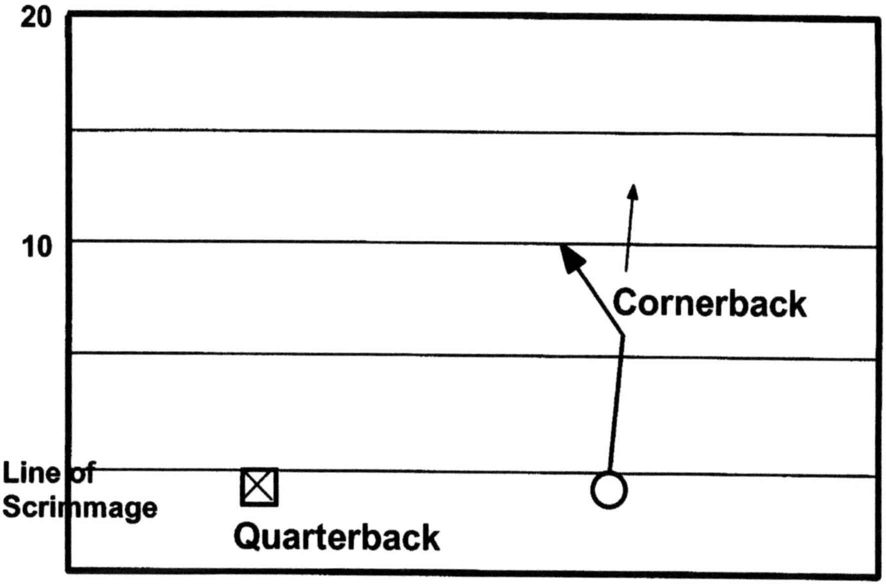

Coaching Points:

- The receiver should burst off the line of scrimmage and run downfield.
- The receiver should make eye contact at a spot right between the defender's eyes.
- The receiver should pump his arms and run at full speed.
- On his third step, the receiver should be at about six-plus yards, and then break (45-degree angle) to the middle of the field using the *pressure step* (outside foot).
- The receiver should run a sharper angle if he has to protect the throw.
- As the receiver snaps his head back to find the quarterback, he should run under control to adjust to a back-hip throw. He should catch the ball at about 11 yards and then immediately break vertically to the goal line.

  √   He should stay on it in all coverages.

12-Yard Speed-Out

Figure 5-5. Route: 3 versus the three-deep zone.

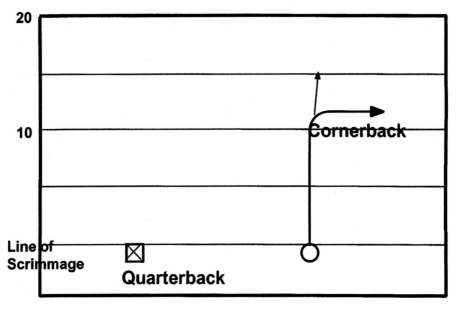

Coaching Points:

- The receiver should burst off the line of scrimmage and run downfield.

- The receiver should make eye contact at a spot right between the defender's eyes.

- At six steps (10-plus yards) the receiver should break to the sideline using the *pressure step* (inside foot) to start his *speed cut*.

- As the receiver snaps his head back to find the quarterback, he should be sure to accelerate out of his break as he finds the ball.

  √ Check the game plan – He can either stay with the route versus press (recommended), or convert the route to a fade.

  √ He should convert the route to a fade versus cover 2, or a rolled-up corner.

12-Yard Curl

Figure 5-6. Route: 4 versus the three-deep zone.

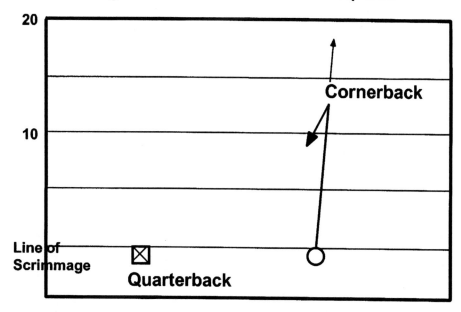

Coaching Points:

- The receiver should burst off the line of scrimmage and run directly at the center of the defender, wherever he is lined up.

- The receiver should make eye contact at a spot right between the defender's eyes.

- The receiver should run at near full speed (do not slow down) and maintain a path directly towards the center of defender regardless of where he tries to go.

- When the receiver's takes his sixth step, he should break down using the *four-step technique*, starting with his inside foot, and ending with a *pressure step* (his outside foot on the tenth step).

- As the receiver snaps his head back to find the quarterback, he should be sure to push off of his *pressure step* and accelerate out of his break as he finds the ball.

  √   He should stay on it in all coverages.

18-Yard Comeback

Figure 5-7. Route: 5 versus the three-deep zone.

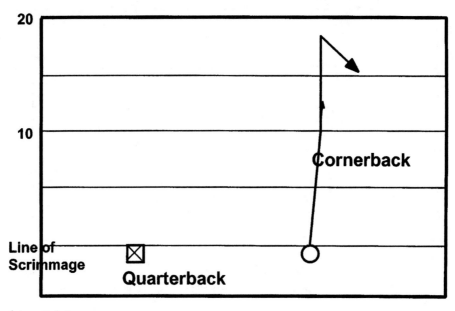

Coaching Points:

- The receiver should burst off the line of scrimmage and run directly at the defender.
- The receiver should make eye contact at a spot right between the defender's eyes.
- With a two-yard cushion, the receiver should make a move past the defender and avoid any contact.
- As the receiver passes the defender (or at 12-plus yards), he should take a vertical stem.
- At 15 yards the receiver should break down using the *four-step technique*, starting with his outside foot, and ending with a *pressure step* (inside foot).
- As the receiver snaps his head back to find the quarterback, he should be sure to push off of his *pressure step* and accelerate out of his break as he finds the ball.

16-Yard Dig

Figure 5-8. Route: 6 versus the three-deep zone.

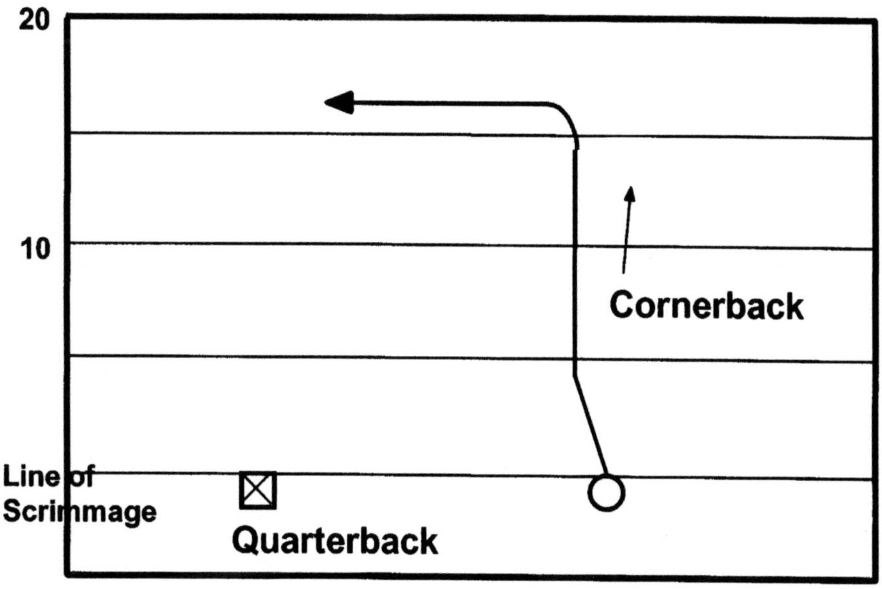

Coaching Points:

- The receiver should burst off the line of scrimmage using a seam release.
- When the receiver gets into the vertical stem of the route, he should make sure to *pop* his route.
- The receiver should run at near full speed (do *not* slow down) and maintain his path.
- At 15-plus yards the receiver should break to the middle using a *pressure step* (outside foot) to start his *speed cut*.
- Depending on where the play is designed to break open, a breakdown cut by the receiver may be appropriate.
- As the receiver snaps his head back to find the quarterback, he should be sure to accelerate out of his break as he finds the hole and the ball.
- The receiver should come *downhill* slightly.

Note: The seam release is used by the single-side wide receiver so that he will break open over the middle of the field *between the tackles*. There will usually be some type of route breaking open underneath the dig route at about four to six yards.

16-Yard Square-In

Figure 5-9. Route: 6 versus the three-deep zone.

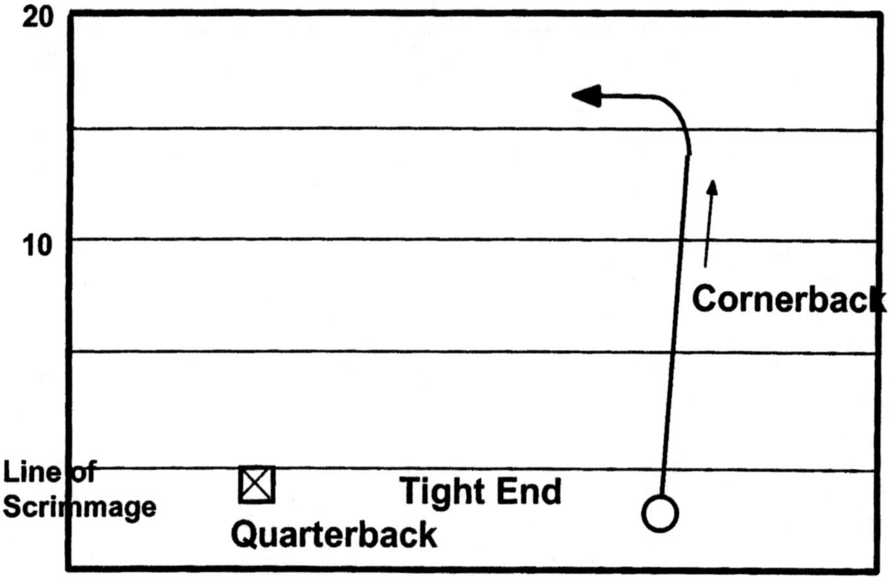

20

10

Cornerback

Line of Scrimmage   ⊠   **Tight End**
Quarterback

Coaching Points:

- The receiver should burst off the line of scrimmage and run downfield.
- The receiver should make eye contact at a spot right between the defender's eyes.
- The receiver should run at near full speed (do *not* slow down) and maintain his path.
- At 14-plus yards the receiver should break to the middle using a *pressure step* (outside foot) to start his *speed cut.*
- As the receiver snaps his head back to find the quarterback, he should be sure to accelerate out of his break as he finds the ball.
- The receiver should come *downhill* slightly.

Note: The ball should be in the air before the receiver makes his break.

12-Yard Post Corner

Figure 5-10. Route: 7 versus the three-deep zone.

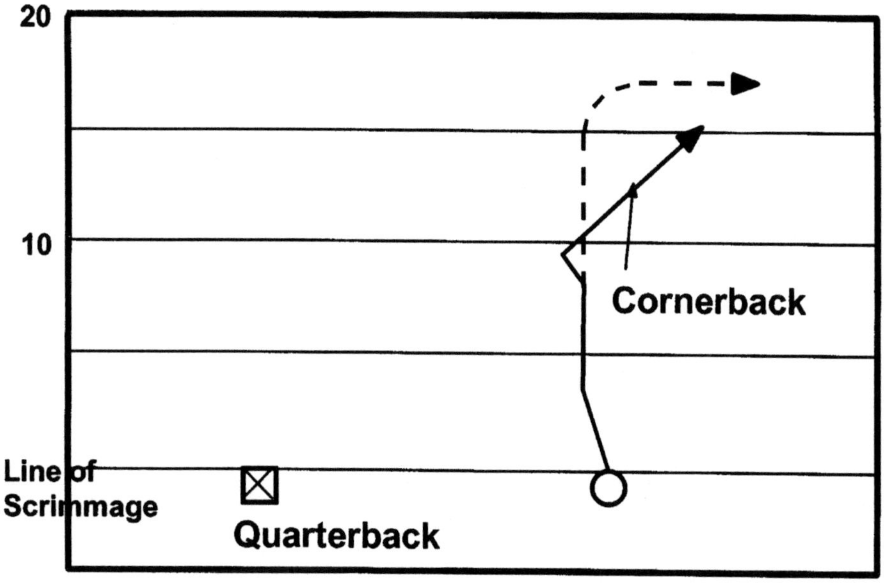

Coaching Points:

- The receiver should burst off the line of scrimmage using an inside seam release (inside foot first).

- On the fourth step the receiver should plant his inside foot at a 45-degree angle (a *pressure step* parallel to the sideline) and snap his head and hips upfield into a vertical stem.

- The receiver should accelerate to threaten deep.

- *Before* he hits nine yards the receiver should break to the post with a *pressure step* (outside foot).

- On his third stride the receiver should use a *pressure step* (inside foot) and break to the corner.

- As the receiver snaps his head back to the quarterback, he should accelerate out of his break.

Note: The ball should be in the air before the receiver makes his break. He shouldn't get too close to the defender before he starts his break – he doesn't want to run into him as he breaks to the corner.

12-Yard Post

Figure 5-11. Route: 8 versus the three-deep zone.

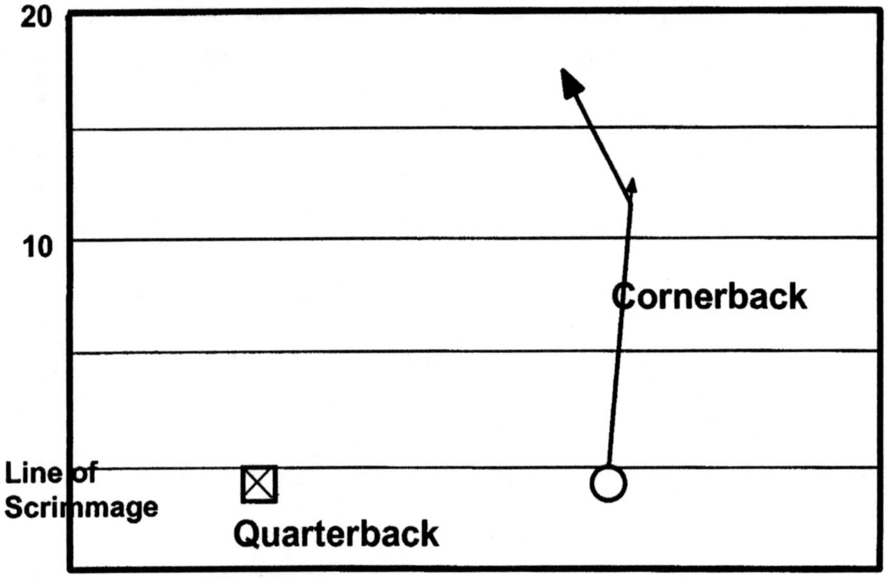

Coaching Points:

*   The receiver should burst off the line of scrimmage and run downfield.
*   The receiver should make eye contact at a spot right between the defender's eyes.
*   The receiver should run at full speed.
*   At 10-plus yards (seven steps) the receiver should break to the middle of the field using a *pressure step* (outside foot) and *pop* his route.
*   As the receiver snaps his head back to find the quarterback, he should be sure to accelerate out of his break as he finds the ball.

Note: As receiver, you should be cognizant of the fact that, as a dropback pass, this is very much a timing route.

Take-Off

Figure 5-12. Route: 9 versus the three-deep zone.

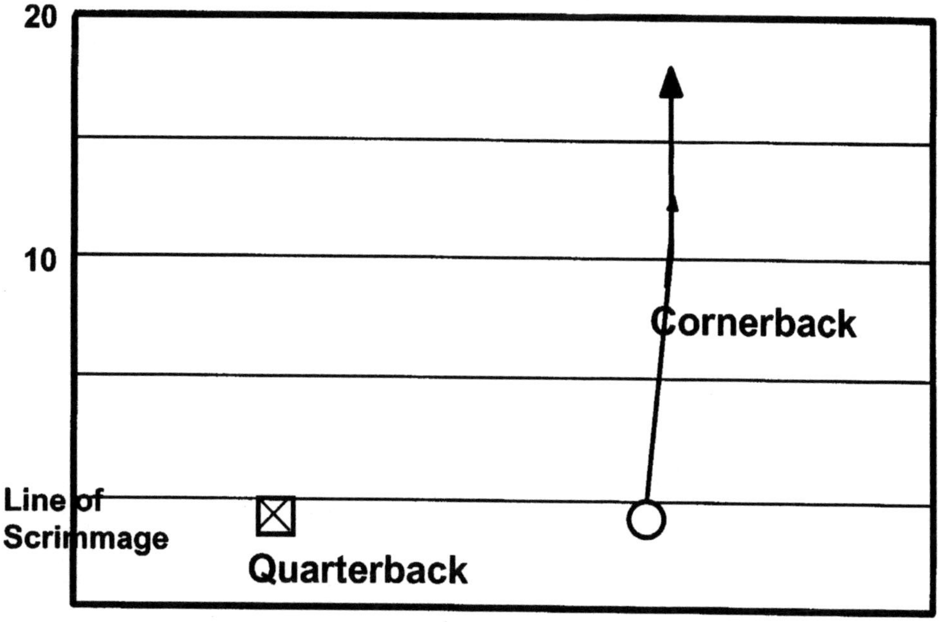

Coaching Points:

- The receiver should burst off the line of scrimmage and run directly at the center of the defender, wherever he is lined up.

- The receiver should make eye contact at a spot right between the defender's eyes.

- The receiver should run at near full speed (do *not* slow down) and maintain a path directly towards the center of defender regardless of where he tries to go.

- With a two-yard cushion, the receiver should make a move past the defender and avoid any contact.

- As the receiver passes the defender (using his hands to knock defender's hands away from him), he should go into a vertical stem.

- The receiver should accelerate and get on top of the defender.

- As the receiver looks back towards the quarterback, he should be sure to accelerate as he finds the ball.

Note: This is a timing pass!

18-Yard Bench

Figure 5-13. Route: Bench versus the three-deep zone.

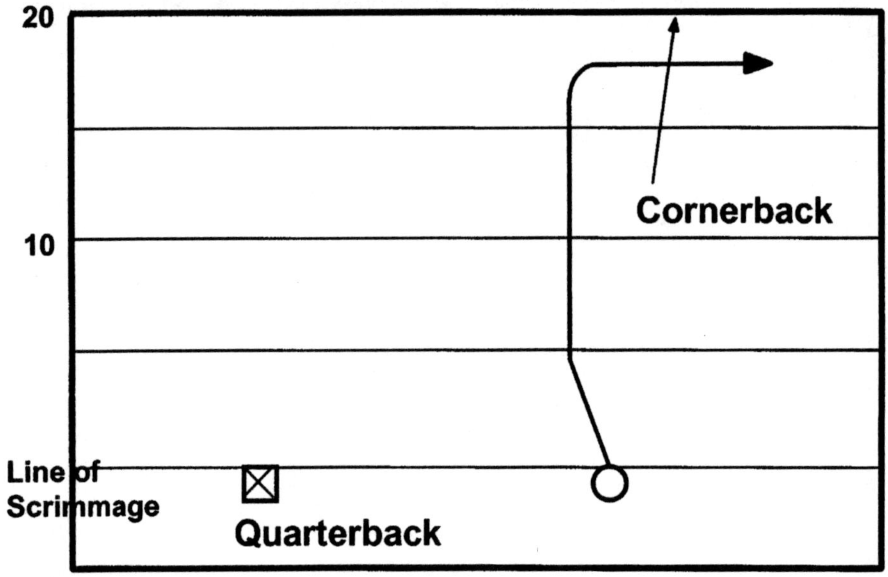

Coaching Points:

- The receiver should burst off the line of scrimmage with an inside release.
- The receiver should use a seam release and *pop* his route as soon as he *glides to threaten deep.*
- At 15 yards the receiver should use a *speed cut*, snapping his head and accelerating to the sideline.
- After making the reception, the receiver should explode vertically to the goal line.

Two-Deep Zone Routes

Cover 2 zone is a zone coverage that consists of five defenders dropping to a depth of 12 yards and covering the field horizontally. Two safeties are responsible for covering the deep zone by splitting the field in half. Each safety is responsible for covering his deep half of the field.

The strengths of the coverage lie in the ability to cover the passing field horizontally up to 12 yards and being able to come up against the run. The weaknesses in this coverage are the deep zone where two safeties are required to cover all deep passes anywhere on the field. The fade area and deep middle area are particularly vulnerable to passes.

Against pass patterns, the cornerback is instructed to *reroute* the receiver to the inside on the receiver's inside-seam release, and then to get to his cover area of the outside flat zone up to 12 yards in depth. Usually if no other receiver or back releases into the cornerback's zone, he will continue to drop deep to the outside quarter of the field.

If the outside receiver takes an outside release, the cornerback is instructed to *reroute* the receiver out of bounds, and then look for another receiver coming into his flat area. If a second receiver or back does not come into his flat area, he will run with the wide receiver much like a man coverage.

Most offenses will run a receiver or back into the flat area to *anchor* the corner to his zone. Therefore, most of your routes will be run to beat the safety on your side. The receiver's primary goal is to find the holes in the defense, make the catch, and then make yardage after the reception.

Figure 5-14.

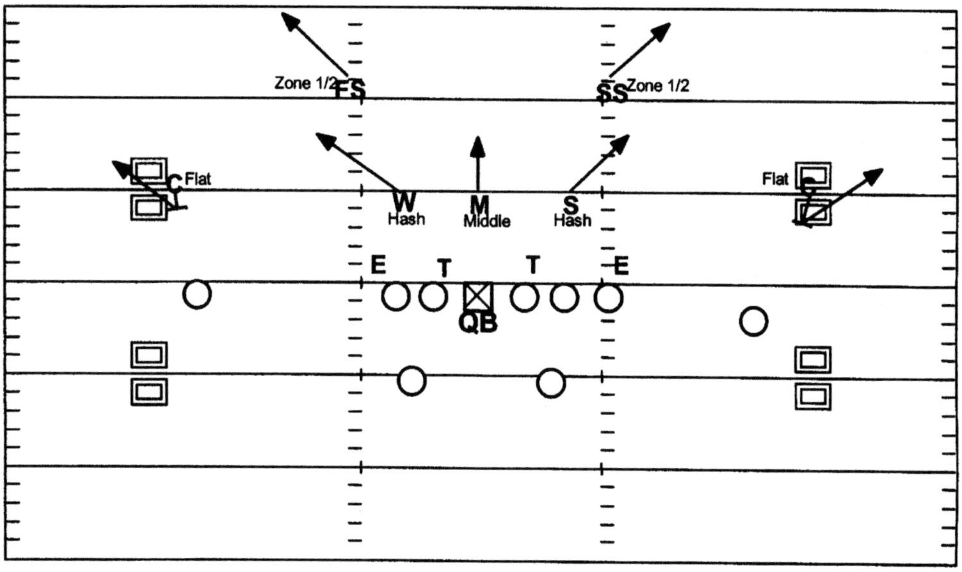

STRENGTHS

1. Five underneath coverage
2. Ability to disrupt timing of outside receivers with 'jam'
3. Can rush four
4. Flat areas

WEAKNESSES

1. Deep coverages;
   a. fade area
   b. deep middle
2. Strong-side curl
3. Run support off-tackle

In cover 2, the corners usually play the receivers at about five-yards off the line of scrimmage, and about one-yard outside. The corner will most likely be looking into the backfield. His primary responsibility is to get a jam on the receiver, and then drop to his coverage area about 12-yards off the line of scrimmage. There will also be three linebackers dropping to the depth of 12 yards. These five defenders cover the field from the line of scrimmage to about 15-yards downfield.

The two safeties will line up near the hash marks and cover half the field from the sideline all the way to their opponent's goal line. In other words, nothing is supposed to get deep on them.

Conversion Routes

Figure 5-15. Routes: Zero, 1, 3, and 9 versus the catch-defenders.

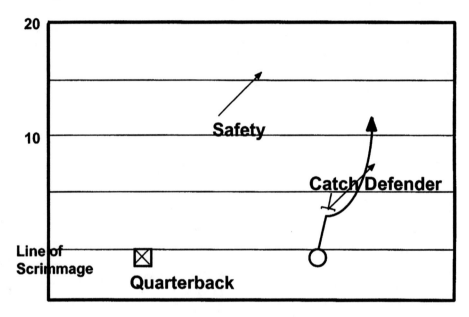

Note: When faced with a catch defender, the following routes will convert to a fade route: "zero"/quick hitch, 1/quick-speed out, 3/ 12-yard speed out, and 9/streak route.

Coaching Points:

- The receiver should burst off the line of scrimmage and run directly at the defender.

- The receiver should make eye contact at a spot right between the defender's eyes.

- The receiver should maintain a path directly towards the center of the defender regardless of where he tries to go.

- The receiver should use moves to get outside of the defender, using his hands to knock the defender's hands away from his body without getting pushed to the sideline.

- As the receiver accelerates past the defender, he should break to a vertical stem and *motor down* as he clears him.
- The receiver should look for the ball *in the hole* before crossing the safety.
- After making the reception, the receiver should explode vertically to the goal line.

Note: If the receiver can not get outside the defender, the receiver can take an inside release (as a last resort) and then bend the route back outside.

Quick Slant

Figure 5-16. Route: 2 versus the catch-defenders.

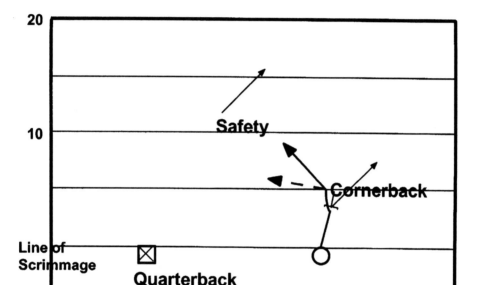

Coaching Points:

- The receiver should burst off the line of scrimmage and run directly at defender.
- At five yards the receiver should plant his outside foot (*pressure step*) and accelerate out of his break to the open area.
- After making the reception, the receiver should explode vertically to the goal line.

Note: The quarterback will put the ball on the receiver's hip – and not lead him into the safety coverage. The receiver may also have to flatten his route to protect the ball from the safety coverage.

12-Yard Curl

Figure 5-17. Route: 4 versus the catch-defenders.

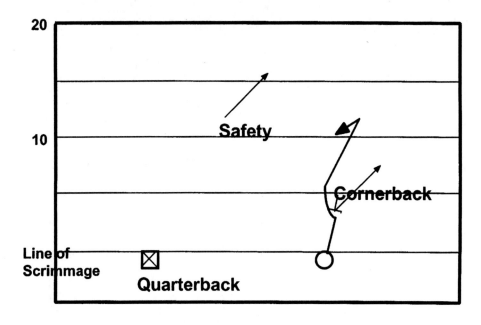

Coaching Points:

- The receiver should burst off the line of scrimmage and run directly at the cornerback.

- When the receiver gets within two to three yards of the defender, he should use a move and get inside the defender, while making sure he uses his hands to keep the defender's hand off of him.

- As the receiver gets by the corner, he should get width back outside into the route.

- At about 10 yards the receiver should break down using the *four-step technique*, starting with his inside foot and ending with a *pressure step* (outside foot).

- As the receiver snaps his head back to find the quarterback, he should be sure to push off his *pressure step* and accelerate out of his break as he finds the ball.

18-Yard Comeback

Figure 5-18. Route: 5 versus the catch-defenders.

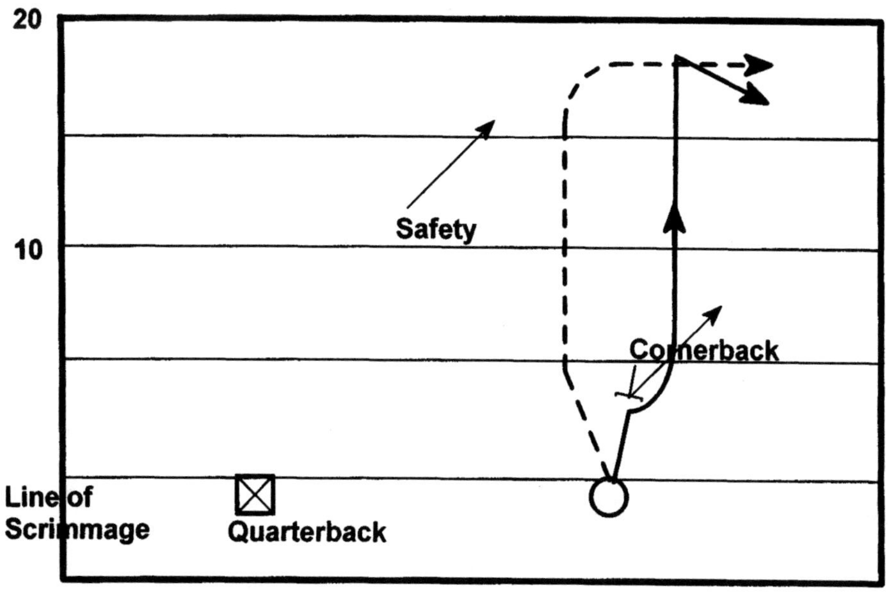

Coaching Points:

- The receiver should burst off the line of scrimmage and run directly at the defender.

- The receiver should make eye contact at a spot right between the defender's eyes.

- The receiver should maintain a path directly towards the center of the defender regardless of where he tries to go.

- The receiver should use moves to get outside of the defender, using his hands to knock the defender's hands away from his body without getting pushed to the sideline.

- As the receiver accelerates past the defender, he should break to a vertical stem.

- At about 15 yards the receiver should break down using the *four-step technique*, starting with his outside foot, and ending with a *pressure step* (inside foot).

- As the receiver snaps his head back to find the quarterback, he should be sure to push off of his *pressure step* and accelerate out of his break as he finds the ball.

Note: Depending on the game plan and the pass pattern, this route could be converted to a *fade* or a *bench* route.

16-Yard Dig

Figure 5-19. Route: 6 versus the catch-defenders.

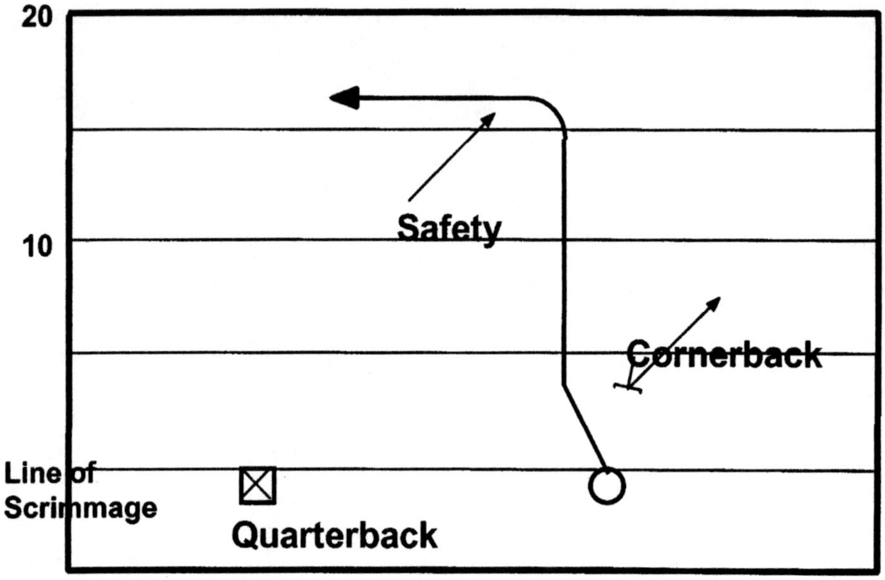

Coaching Points:

- The receiver should burst off the line of scrimmage using an inside-seam release.
- The receiver should snap his hips on a vertical stem.
- The receiver should run directly at the safety's outside shoulder looking past him.
- At 14 yards the receiver should use a *speed cut* to get underneath the safety.
- The receiver should look for the ball at *glide speed* and come *downhill* slightly.
- After making the reception, the receiver should explode vertically to the goal line.

Note: The dig route is run by the single-side receiver.

16-Yard Square-In

Figure 5-20. Route: 6 versus the catch-defenders.

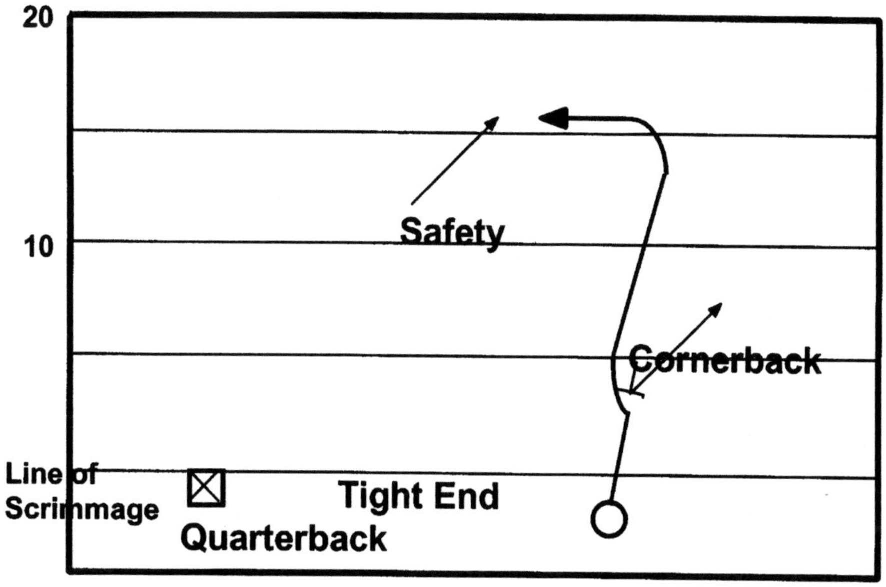

Coaching Points:

- The receiver should burst off the line of scrimmage and run directly at the cornerback.

- When the receiver gets within two to three yards of the defender, he should use a move and get inside the defender, while making sure he uses his hands to keep the defender's hand off of him.

- As the receiver gets by corner, he should get width back outside into the route.

- At 14 yards the receiver should use a *speed cut* to get underneath the safety.

- The receiver should look for the ball at *glide speed* and come *downhill* slightly.

- After making the reception, the receiver should explode vertically to the goal line.

Note: The square-in is usually run by the outside receiver on the two-receiver side. He needs to widen his route to open up a passing lane for the quarterback.

12-Yard Post-Corner

Figure 5-21. Route: 7 versus the catch-defenders.

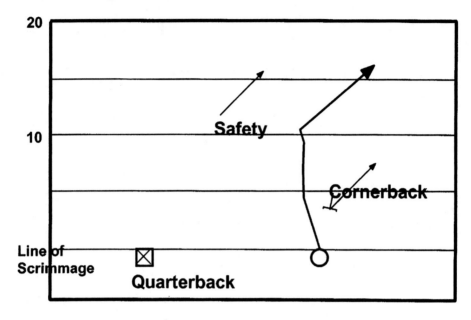

Coaching Points:

- The receiver should burst off the line of scrimmage using an inside-seam release.
- The receiver should snap his hips on a vertical stem.
- The receiver should run vertically at near full speed looking past the safety.
- At nine yards the receiver should break to the post using a *pressure step* (outside foot).
- On his third step the receiver should break to the corner using a *pressure step* (inside foot).
- As the receiver accelerates out of his break, he should snap his head back towards the quarterback to find the ball.

Note: Situations will arise when the post move is not necessary. Sometimes the safety is so far inside that the inside break isn't necessary – just leave him inside.

12-Yard Post

Figure 5-22. Route: 8 versus the catch-defenders.

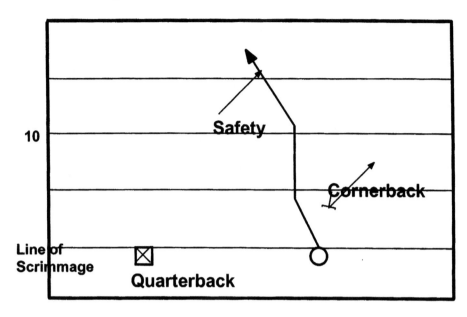

Coaching Points:

- The receiver should burst off the line of scrimmage using an inside-seam release.
- The receiver should snap his hips on a vertical stem.
- The receiver should run vertically at near full speed looking past the safety.
- At 12 yards the receiver should break to the post using a *pressure step* (outside foot) and split the safeties.
- As the receiver accelerates out of his break, he should snap his head back towards the quarterback to find the ball.

18-Yard Bench

Figure 5-23. Route: Bench versus the catch-defenders.

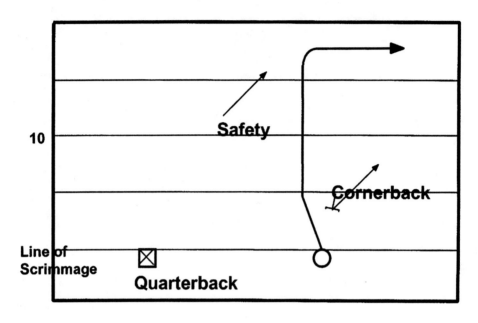

Coaching Points:

- The receiver should burst off the line of scrimmage using an inside-seam release.
- The receiver should snap his hips on a vertical stem.
- The receiver should run vertically at near full speed looking past the safety.
- At 15 yards the receiver should break to the sideline using a *pressure step* (inside foot) to start his *speed cut*.
- As the receiver snaps his head back to find the quarterback, he should be sure to accelerate out of his break as he finds the ball.

Note: The cornerback will be anchored in the flat with a back running into the flat. The *bench* is also used as an adjustment to the 18-yard comeback route.

Man-Off Routes

Receivers who run routes against man-off defenders probably have the best opportunity to utilize all the tools in their arsenal. At the same time however, the defense is most likely bringing extra people on the rush, so it is imperative that the receivers run their routes quickly and efficiently.

Receivers can use any number of releases when going against man-off defenders. They must be cognizant of the other routes being run in the pattern to best utilize the field spacing necessary in the modern passing game.

Eye Focus

One of the most accessible tools to use against a defender in man-off coverage is the receiver's eye-focus. When running the pass route, the receiver should focus at a point directly between the defenders eyes. Many times, the receiver will unconsciously look into the defender's eye on the side he is about to break to. This is a tip that will give the defender an advantage in coverage.

Whenever a defense goes into any kind of man coverage, the offense can expect some type of blitz. Crossing routes can be very productive versus a cover 1 free, provided the offense has the extra rusher(s) blocked. In addition, fade routes run by the outside receivers, or even 4-vertical patterns run by the receivers, can be big plays as long as the ball is thrown away from the free safety (Figure 5-24).

Figure 5-24.

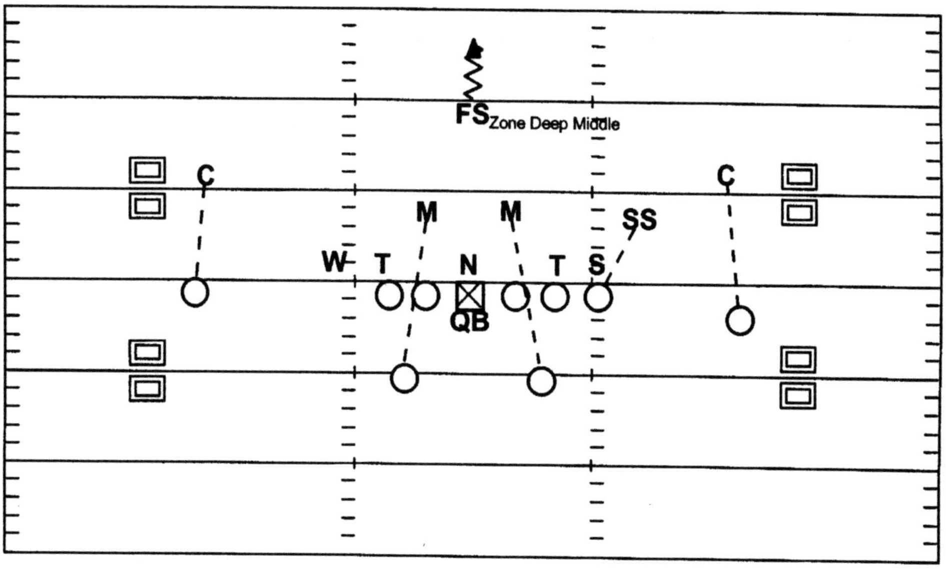

STRENGTHS	WEAKNESSES
1. Help in the deep middle	1. No underneath help
2. Tight coverage	a. crossing routes
3. Good run support to SS	b. breaking routes
4. Can rush five	c. pick routes
	2. Play action passes
	3. Out routes

The offense can expect more rushers than it can block with conventional pass protection versus a cover zero man. Some teams bring seven or even eight defenders once in a while. Although this is fundamentally unsound because they can't have all the possible receivers accounted for, it can cause a big play defensively if the offense attempts to drop back and wait for one of the receivers to break open downfield. Again, crossing routes are effective as well as routes the are run vertically down the field as long as you can get the pass off before the rush gets to you (Figure 5-25).

Figure 5-25.

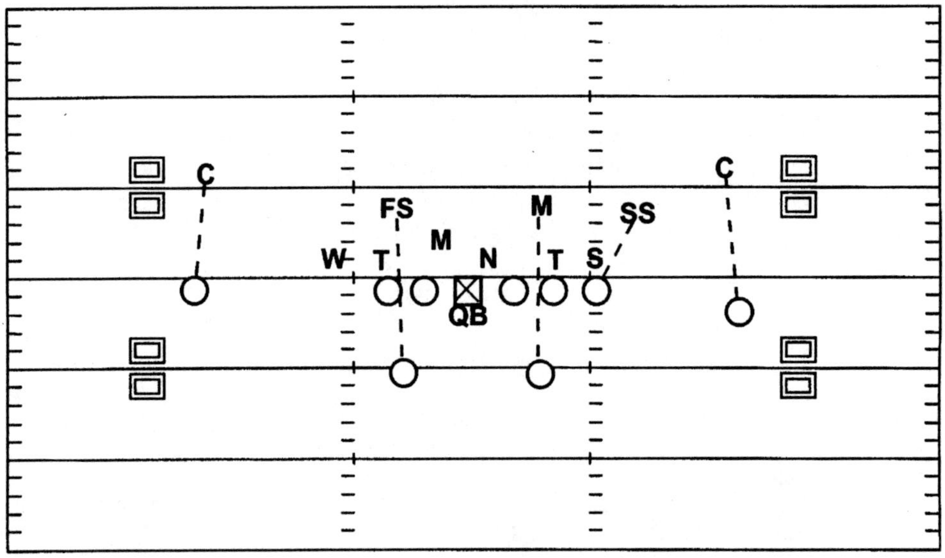

STRENGTHS

1. Pass rush

2. Can rush six or more

3. Tight coverage

4. Good run support

WEAKNESSES

1. No underneath help

   a. crossing routes

   b. breaking routes

   c. pick routes

2. Nobody in the middle of the field

   a. deep post route

Quick Hitch

Figure 5-26. Route: Zero versus the man-off defenders.

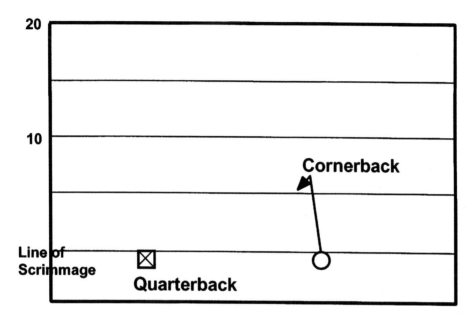

Coaching Points:

- The receiver should burst off the line of scrimmage and run downfield attacking the defender wherever he lines up (remember he does not want to get beat deep).

- The receiver should begin his breakdown on the fourth (inside foot) step and pivot on the fifth *pressure step.*

- As the receiver snaps his head back to find the quarterback, he should be sure to be a stationary target for the quarterback as he finds the ball – he shouldn't drift from the ball.

- After securing the ball, the receiver should take a jab step inside and break to the outside (usually).

Quick Speed

Figure 5-27. Route: 1 versus the man-off defenders.

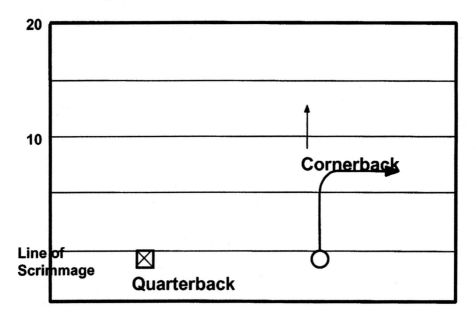

Coaching Points:

- The receiver should burst off the line of scrimmage and run straight downfield unless the defender has an outside technique (if he has an outside technique, the receiver should run directly at the center of the defender, wherever he is lined up).

- The receiver should make eye contact at a spot right between the defender's eyes.

- The receiver should run at near full speed (do *not* slow down) and run directly downfield (unless the defender has an outside technique – then the receiver should maintain a path directly towards the center of defender regardless of where he tries to go).

- At five-plus yards the receiver should break to the sideline using a *pressure step* (inside foot) to start his *speed cut*.

- As the receiver snaps his head back to find the quarterback, he should be sure to accelerate out of his break as he finds the ball.

Quick Slant

Figure 5-28. Route: 2 versus the man-off defenders.

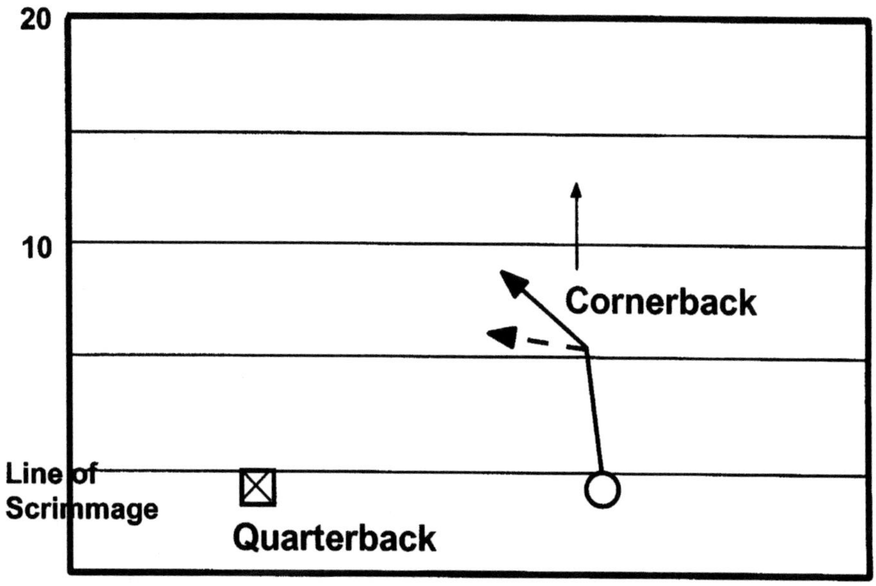

Coaching Points:

- The receiver should burst off the line of scrimmage and run directly at the center of the defender, wherever he is lined up.

- The receiver should make eye contact at a spot right between the defender's eyes.

- The receiver should run at full speed and maintain a path directly towards the center of defender regardless of where he tries to go.

- At six-plus yards the receiver should break to the inside of the defender using a *pressure step* (outside foot) and head upfield.

- As the receiver snaps his head back to find the quarterback, he should be sure to accelerate out of his break as he finds the ball. He should catch the ball at about 11-yards out.

Note: The quarterback will put the ball on the receiver's hip – and not lead him into the safety coverage. The receiver may also have to flatten his route to protect the ball from the safety coverage.

12-Yard Speed Out

Figure 5-29. Route: 3 versus the man-off defenders.

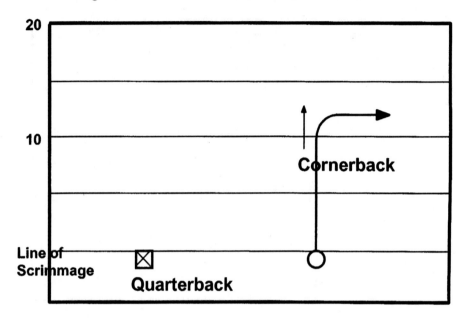

Coaching Points:

- The receiver should burst off the line of scrimmage and run straight downfield unless the defender has an outside technique (if he has an outside technique, the receiver should run directly at the center of the defender, wherever he is lined up).

- The receiver should make eye contact at a spot right between the defender's eyes.

- The receiver should run at near full speed (do *not* slow down), and run directly downfield (unless the defender has an outside technique – then the receiver should maintain a path directly towards the center of the defender regardless of where he tries to go).

- At ten-plus yards the receiver should break to the sideline using a *pressure step* (inside foot) to start his *speed cut.*

- As the receiver snaps his head back to find the quarterback, he should be sure to accelerate out of his break as he finds the ball.

12-Yard Curl

Figure 5-30. Route: 4 versus the man-off defenders.

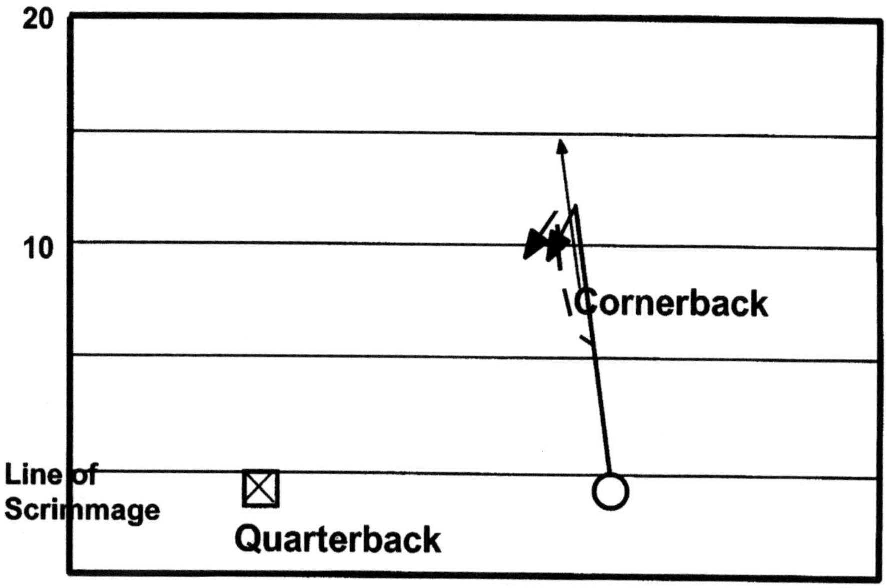

Coaching Points:

- The receiver should burst off the line of scrimmage and run directly at the center of the defender, wherever he is lined up.

- The receiver should make eye contact at a spot right between the defender's eyes.

- The receiver should run at near full speed (do not slow down) and maintain a path directly towards the center of the defender regardless of where he tries to go.

- Once the receiver takes his sixth step, he should break down using the *four-step technique*, starting with his inside foot, and ending with a *pressure step* (his outside foot on the tenth step).

- As the receiver snaps his head back to find the quarterback, he should be sure to push off of his *pressure step* and accelerate out of his break as he finds the ball.

Note: If the defender sits on the route, the receiver should explode into his inside shoulder, push vertically upfield, and then come back to the football, using his body to shield the defender from the pass.

18-Yard Comeback

Figure 5-31. Route: 5 versus the man-off defenders.

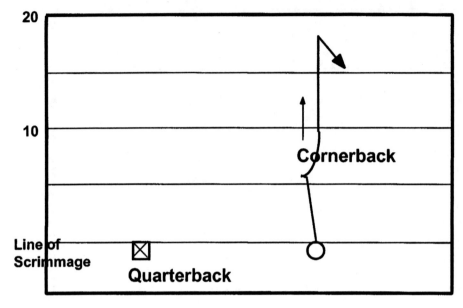

Coaching Points:

- The receiver should burst off the line of scrimmage and run directly at the center of the defender, wherever he is lined up.

- The receiver should make eye contact at a spot right between the defender's eyes.

- The receiver should run full speed downfield (do *not* slow down) and maintain a path directly towards the center of defender regardless of where he tries to go.

- With a two-yard cushion the receiver should make a move past the defender to the outside and avoid any contact.

- As the receiver passes the defender, he should redirect into a vertical stem forcing the defender to turn his hips parallel to the sideline.

- At 15 yards the receiver should break down using the *four-step technique*, starting with his outside foot, and ending with a *pressure step* (inside foot).

- As the receiver snaps his head back to find the quarterback, he should be sure to push off his *pressure step* and accelerate out of his break as he finds the ball.

Note: The receiver should never take an inside release.

16-Yard Dig

Figure 5-32. Route: 6 versus the man-off defenders.

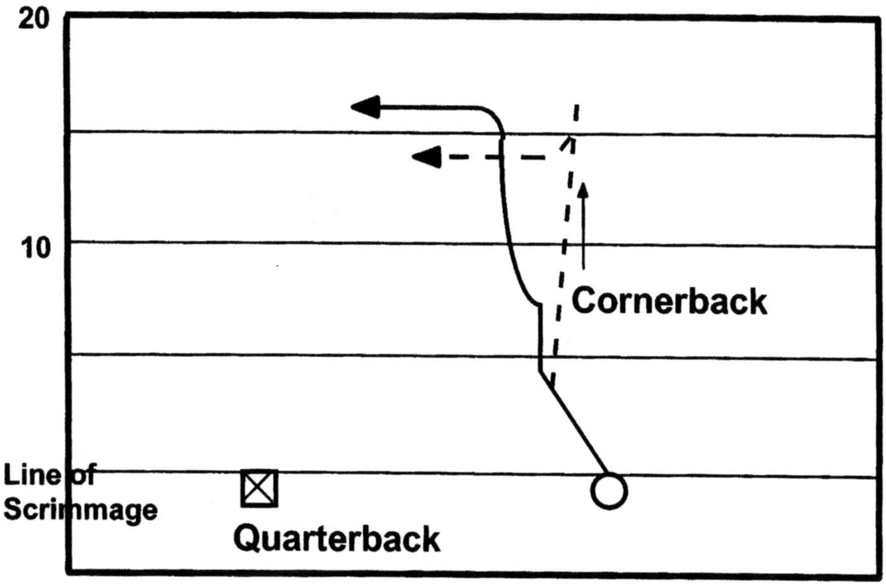

Coaching Points:

- The receiver should burst off the line of scrimmage using a seam release.
- The receiver should get the inside leverage on the defender and vertically push him upfield if possible.
- The receiver should run at full speed (do *not* slow down) and maintain a vertical path.
- At 15-plus yards the receiver should break to the middle using a *pressure step* (outside foot) to start his *speed cut*.
- The receiver should consider using a breakdown cut or a *top gun* move.
- As the receiver snaps his head back to find the quarterback, he should be sure to accelerate out of his break as he finds a hole and the ball.
- The receiver should come *downhill* slightly.

Note: If the defender walls off the inside, the receiver may want to use a *top gun* move to break underneath him. If the receiver has superior speed, he can go over the top of the defender. The seam release is used by the single-side wide receiver so that he will break open over the middle of the field *between the tackles*. Some type of route will usually break open underneath the dig route at about four to six yards.

16-Yard Square

Figure 5-33. Route: 6 versus the man-off defenders.

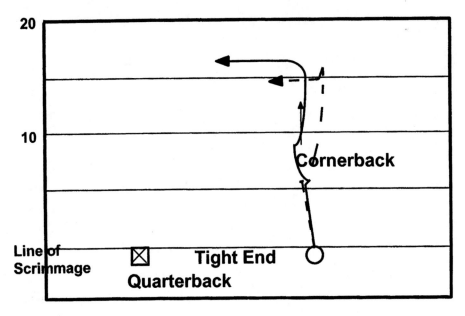

Coaching Points:

- The receiver should burst off the line of scrimmage and attack the defender (make sure he takes a wide split, because he has another receiver inside of him).

- The route should open outside in the first window, so the receiver should do what he can to influence the defender to the outside.

- If the defender gets inside the receiver, he should be sure to push the defender vertically and widen the space between them before breaking to the middle of the field.

- If the defender won't give the receiver the inside, he should push the defender upfield and use a *top gun* move to get under him.

- At about 15 yards the receiver should break to the middle and snap his head back towards the quarterback to find the football.

- The receiver should come downhill slightly.

12-Yard Post Corner

Figure 5-34. Route: 7 versus the man-off defenders.

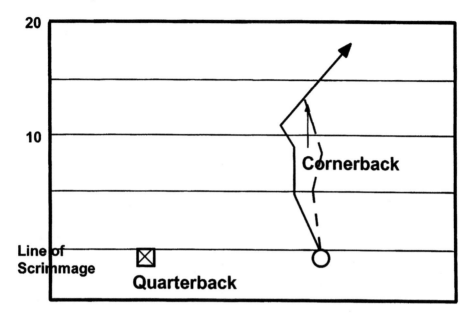

Coaching Points:

- The receiver should burst off the line of scrimmage using an inside-seam release.
- The receiver should snap his hips on a vertical stem.
- The receiver should run vertically at near full speed looking past the safety.
- At nine yards the receiver should break to the post using a *pressure step* (outside foot).
- On his third step the receiver should break to the corner using a *pressure step* (inside foot).
- As the receiver accelerates out of his break, he should snap his head back towards the quarterback to find the ball.

Note: If the defender tries to jam the receiver at about 10 yards, the receiver should get outside leverage on him, lean on him, and then accelerate to the corner.

12-Yard Post

Figure 5-35. Route: 8 versus the man-off defenders.

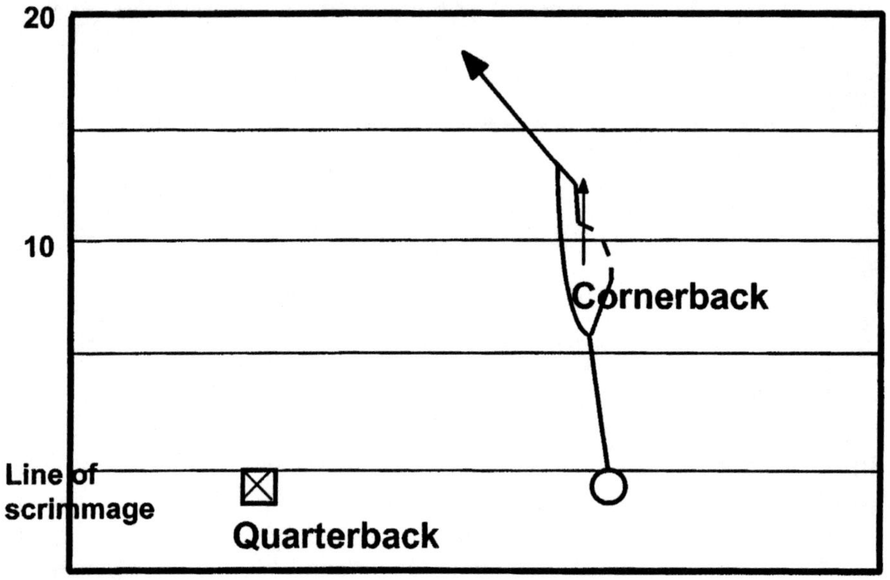

Coaching Points:

- The receiver should burst off the line of scrimmage using an attack release.
- The receiver should get the inside leverage on the defender and vertically push him upfield.
- The receiver should run at full speed (do *not* slow down) and maintain a vertical path.
- At 10-plus yards the receiver should break to the post using the *stick move* (outside foot), and then accelerate downfield.
- As the receiver snaps his head back to find the quarterback, he should be sure to accelerate out of his break as he finds a hole and the ball.

Note: If the receiver has superior speed, or catches the defender squared-up on his heels, the receiver may go over the top of him, but he must lean into the defender as he goes over the top, and then stick to his route as he accelerates away.

Take-Off

Figure 5-36. Route: 9 versus the three-deep zone.

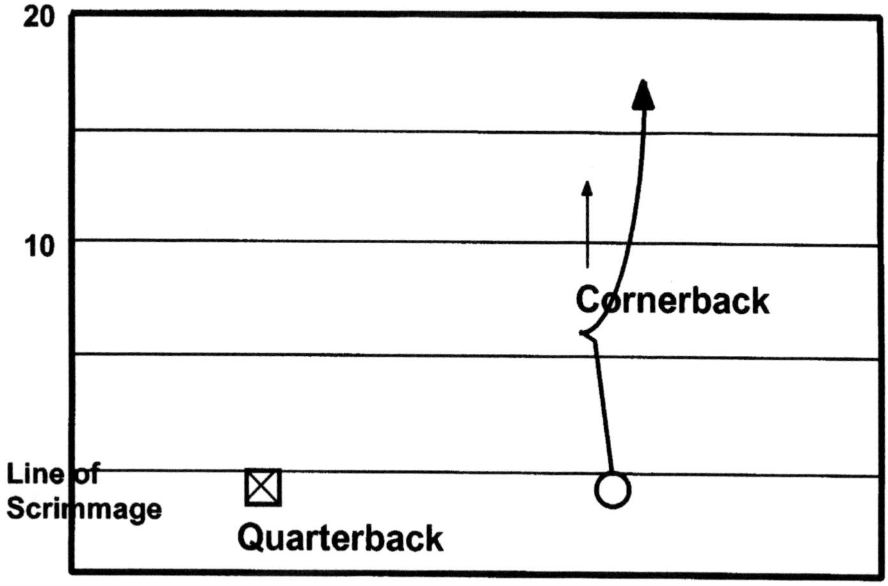

Coaching Points:

- The receiver should burst off the line of scrimmage and run directly at the center of the defender, wherever he is lined up.

- The receiver should make eye contact at a spot right between the defender's eyes.

- The receiver should run at near full speed (do *not* slow down) and maintain a path directly towards the center of defender regardless of where he tries to go.

- With a two-yard cushion, the receiver should move past the defender and avoid any contact.

- As the receiver passes the defender (using his hands to knock defender's hands away from him), he should go into a vertical stem.

- The receiver should accelerate and get on top of the defender.

- As the receiver looks back towards the quarterback, he should be sure to accelerate as he finds the ball.

Note: This is a timing pass!

18-Yard Bench

Figure 5-37. Route: Bench versus the man-off defenders.

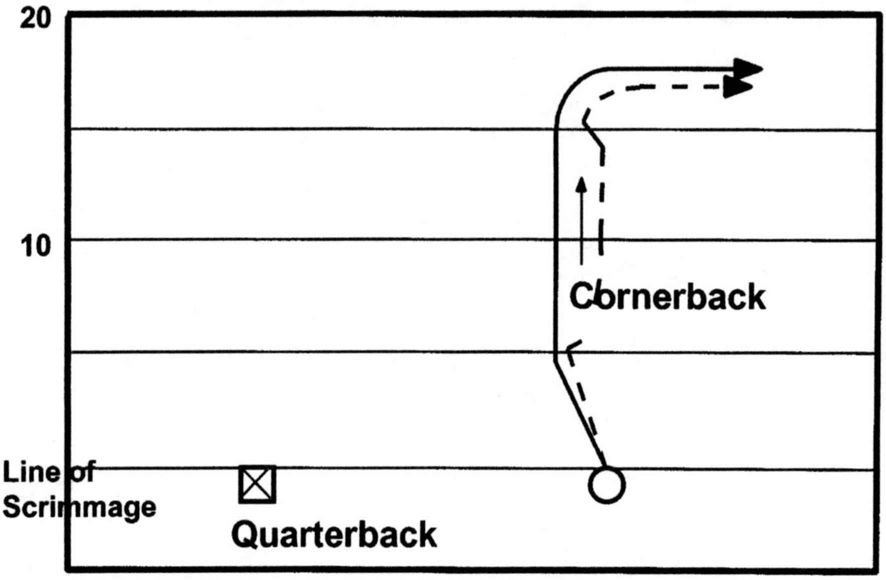

Coaching Points:

- The receiver should burst off the line of scrimmage using an inside-seam release.
- The receiver should snap his hips on a vertical stem.
- The receiver should run vertically at near full speed looking past the safety.
- At 15 yards the receiver should break to the sideline using a *pressure step* (inside foot) to start his *speed cut*.
- As the receiver snaps his head back to find the quarterback, he should be sure to accelerate out of his break as he finds the ball.

Note: If the cornerback won't let the receiver inside, he should go vertically outside him, lean him in, and then stick him as he breaks to the sideline.

CHAPTER 6

Techniques Used Versus Bump-and-Run Defenders

Running pass routes against bump-and-run defenders can be very productive for both the receiver and the offense — if the receiver knows what the defenders are trained to do, as well as how to defeat them. Most often the defensive back is instructed to take away the inside release of the receiver so that the receiver has great difficulty running inside pass patterns. If however the receiver does get inside the defensive back, the defensive back is taught to get on the inside hip of the receiver, thereby taking away most inside routes. Many defenses assume that offenses will convert their pass route to a fade route when confronted with bump-and-run defenders. The fade route is one of the lowest (if not the lowest) percentage pass routes in all of football. However, in certain situations with the right matchup, the fade route is very appropriate.

The defensive back also assumes that the receiver will take the release that will get him to his area for receiving the ball the quickest — e.g., the receiver will take an inside release to run an inside route and will take an outside release to run an outside route. In addition, many times the defender is instructed to disrupt the receiver with a *jam* at the line of scrimmage just after the ball is snapped. This technique can be very effective in getting the receiver out of his game. Even though holding the receiver by his jersey or pads is technically illegal, the technique is extremely effective and can kill the route. The receiver must use his hands to knock the defender's hands away *before* the defensive back can grab his jersey.

The following are effective strategies in defeating bump-and-run defenders. Three basic elements of defeating the bump-and-run coverage are the *stance* versus bump-and-run defenders, the *release* versus the bump-and-run defenders, and using the hands and arms to disrupt the bump-and-run defenders. Also included are the individual routes and techniques involved in running those routes effectively.

The Stance

The receiver's feet should be staggered front to back and should have a comfortable lateral separation so as to execute an effective start (See Chapter 1). His feet should still be fairly close together, usually slightly farther than heel-to-toe. His posture should be almost erect and he should never be leaning into the defender. His hands can be brought up to chest level so he will able to knock the defender's hands away at the snap of the ball (Figure 6-1). This stance allows the receiver to be in the most advantageous position to execute a quick release versus the bump-and-run defender.

Figure 6-1. The stance.

- The receiver's hands are in a good position, at chest level, so he can knock the defender's hands away should he attempt to jam him.

- Against a bump-and-run defender, the receiver should bring his feet closer together because his first step will be lateral rather than forward.

It is important that the receiver narrow his stance when confronted with bump-and-run defenders, because he must be able to get into his lateral move(s) or his diagonal escape release more quickly than usual. This will be crucial so the receiver can get the downfield push he needs to run his routes and maintain the timing of the offense.

Most receivers will instinctively try to get lower in their stance and lean into the defender. This will actually make it easier for the defender to jam the receiver, because the receiver is now closer to the defender. When the receiver stands more erect, he is in a better position to knock the defender's hands away when there is an attempted jam. The receiver is also in a better position to move laterally (using moves to get the defender to jump out of the receiver's running lane) in order to get past the defender, and get downfield as quickly as possible.

Releases

The type of release used will depend on the type of bump-and-run defender the receiver is facing. Four types of releases will be covered in this section: the speed release, the single-step release, the double-step release, and the fade-break release.

The Speed Release

The speed release works very well when the receiver has greater speed than the defender, and can basically run away from the coverage. The following example illustrates a receiver taking an outside speed release (Figure 6-2). He can use this release on a number of different routes depending on several factors that can include: how he matches up against the defender, the specific route the receiver is going to run, and how the receiver intends to manipulate or set up the defender. The technique is simple: the receiver picks a side to release to and moves quickly as he explodes off the line of scrimmage and runs downfield.

Figure 6-2. The speed release.

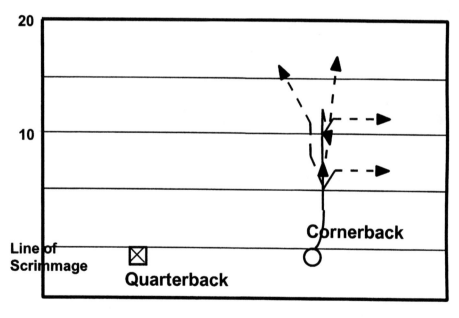

The Single-Step Release

This release is probably used more than any other release as far as bump-and-run coverage is concerned (Figure 6-3). This release should be used primarily when the receiver has a physical or psychological advantage over the defender. Since the defender is seeing this type of release more than any other, both at practice and in games, he may feel fairly comfortable covering receivers who use move.

Figure 6-3. The single-step release.

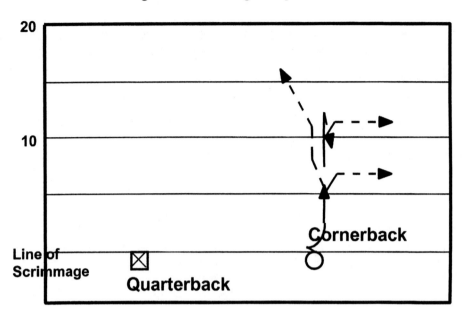

The basic purpose of this move is to gain a step on the defender to leave him behind when releasing downfield (Figure 6-4). However, a good defender will ignore this first move, and jump on the second. At certain times this type of release can move the defender out of the receiver's running lane (assuming the receiver is extremely quick) and allow him a step or two head start downfield. By mixing up releases, this single-step release can be quite effective.

Figure 6-4.

• The single-step release is executed behind the line of scrimmage to get the defender to *lean* to the opposite side the receiver is releasing to.

• The line of scrimmage is here.

The Double-Step Release

If the receiver is fairly quick, this type of release can be most effective; *where you want to go, where you don't want to go, where you want to go*. This means that starting with the foot at the side the receiver wants to release to, he will begin the move. For example, let's assume the receiver wants to take an outside release. With the foot on the side he wants to release to, he will take a jab step in that direction without crossing the line of scrimmage. Then, he takes his inside foot and takes a jab step towards the inside of the defender, again without crossing the line of scrimmage -- but not so far inside that his feet are more than 18-inches apart, which would cause him to lose his leverage. Finally, with the outside foot, the receiver will drive to the outside of the defender upfield quickly and efficiently (Figures 6-5 and 6-6).

This is an effective move because most receivers only use a single-step release and the defender almost always jumps on the second move. This technique takes hours to develop, but once learned, it will allow the receiver to beat any defender off the line of scrimmage.

Figure 6-5. The double-step release.

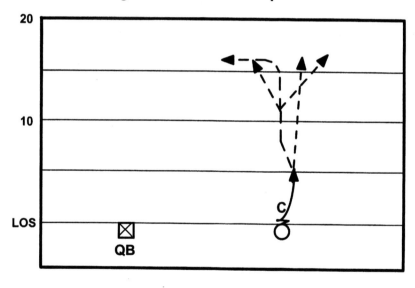

This double-step release allows the receiver to separate from the defender and get on top of him as far as the route is concerned. This is used primarily if the receiver wants to beat the defender downfield, or if the receiver wants to get to the inside of the defender while separating from him as well.

Figure 6-6.

- The double-step release creates the greatest initial separation at the line of scrimmage.

- It is important that the receiver remember to use his hands to knock down the defender's attempt to grab, or disrupt, the receiver's route.

- The double-step release is executed behind the line of scrimmage.

The Fade-Break Release

The fade-break release is used to get underneath a defender when a slant pass is called (Figure 6-7). The receiver starts outside with three hard steps. Then on the third step, he will plant and throw the defender off, and break upfield quickly before breaking for the ball.

Figure 6-7. The fade-break release.

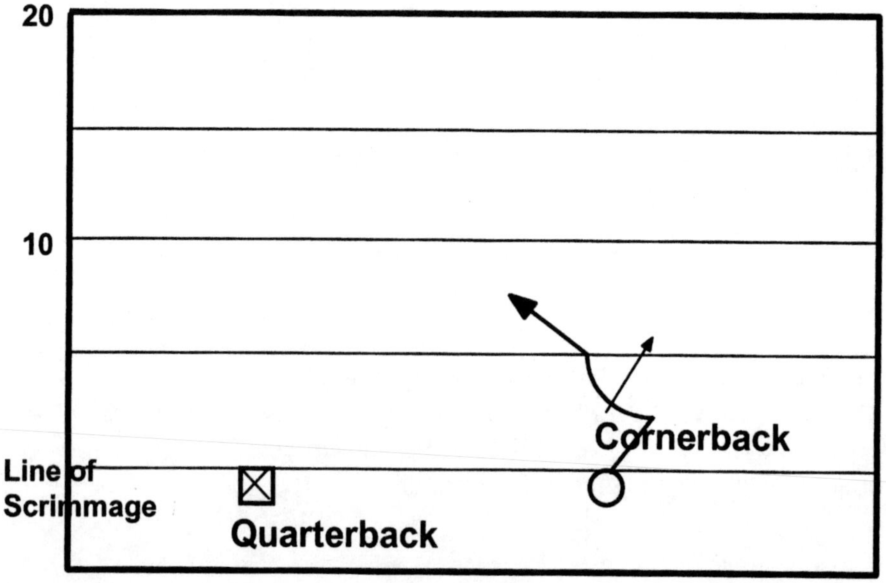

This is very effective when the receiver is primarily using outside releases. The defender does not expect this kind of move and allows the receiver to break open quite easily, and creates the most separation just before the ball gets in the air. It should be noted that it is never acceptable for the receiver to use an outside release to run a quick-slant route.

The Use of Hands

One of the most effective techniques of the bump-and-run releases is for the receiver to aggressively use his hands and arms to knock the defender's hands off of his body. This prevents the defender from holding on to the receiver's jersey to disrupt his route. When the ball is snapped, the receiver will swipe at the defender's hands as the defender reaches out to jam or grab the receiver. The receiver can also either come down hard with a chopping motion towards the defender's wrists, or the receiver can rip upwards with his arm raised up towards his helmet, ripping away much like a boxer is instructed to block an opponent's punch. It is important to remember that many times one swipe to knock the defender's hands away is not enough; the receiver may have to continuously use the slap or rip motion several times while running the route. Also, the receiver should always bring his onside leg through when he is using the *hammer* move, *ripping, slapping,* or *swimming,* so he will have good leverage on the defender throughout the release (Figure 6-8).

Figure 6-8.

Finally, the defender is initially defeated *behind the line of scrimmage,* and so the receiver must be patient yet quick with his moves. The key to beating the bump-and-run defender is a fairly clean release and a good crisp vertical stem in the route. To do this takes practice and patience. The more the receiver works on these areas, the easier they are to apply *automatically.*

The Hammer

The *hammer* is a technique where the receiver will attack the defender's arms by swinging his clinched fist and forearm downward (like a hammer) and hitting the defender's extended arm(s) before he can grab the receiver's jersey. This motion must be done quickly and with great force if it is to have the desired affect (Figure 6-9).

The *hammer* technique usually keeps the defender from grabbing the receiver's jersey for two primary reasons. First, the defender's hands are knocked away from the receiver before the defender can get his hands close enough to grab the receiver's jersey. Second, the force of the receiver's arm coming down on the defender's extended arms causes pain to the defender. The more pain inflicted, the less likely the defender will continue this type of behavior.

Figure 6-9.

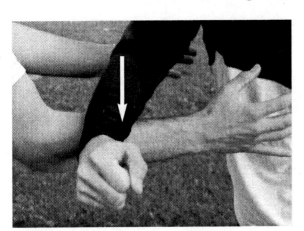

- The receiver's arm is coming down hard on the defender's outstretched arms before the defender can grab the receiver's jersey.

The Rip

Using the *rip* is less aggressive than using the *hammer* but can still be very effective. Basically, the receiver is getting his defender-side arm below the defenders hands, and then ripping upward and outward, away from his body. This action pushes the defender's hands up and out of the way of the receiver, allowing the receiver to push the defender behind him. The rip is more of a finesse move that must be initiated quickly, but is a very good change-up during a game. Defensive linemen also use this move quite often when they pass rush. The key is to get under the defensive back's leverage in relation to the receiver (Figure 6-10).

The Slap

The *slap* is a hand move that is usually used in conjunction with the other hand moves. The main thing is for the receiver to get his hands in contact with the defender's hands *before* the defender can hit or grab the receiver. The slap is usually initiated from just above belt-level. The receiver takes his hand that is furthest from the defender, and slaps at the defender's hand as he attempts to disrupt the receiver's movement upfield (Figure 6-11).

As a secondary hand move, the *slap* works great. Once the primary hand move is executed, the slap is used to make sure the defender does not get a hand on the receiver. This technique also helps the receiver get by the defender and into the pass route.

Figure 6-10.

- The receiver is ripping upward with his right arm blocking the defender's hands before the defender can grab the receiver's jersey.

Figure 6-11.

- The receiver is slapping the defender's outstretched arms away before the defender can grab the receiver's jersey or jam the receiver.

The Swim

The *swim* move is very common and used primarily by taller receivers who are being defended by shorter corners. However, when used incorrectly, the swim move can leave the receiver in a very vulnerable and off-balanced position. The most important point is for the receiver to get his feet in a balanced position while executing the swim move.

The receiver will bring his defender-side arm up over the defender, and then down and away, much like the motion used when swimming using a freestyle technique. When the receiver brings his defender-side arm up, he will use the *slap* technique with his *off* hand before bringing his onside arm down (Figure 6-12).

It is critical that the receiver bring his defender-side foot through (out in front of) the defender. This is because the offside foot can be used to balance the receiver if he should he get pushed outside by the defender. It usually feels awkward when first learning this technique, but it will allow the receiver to drive vertically upfield past the defender and prevent him from getting pushed outside.

Figure 6-12.

- The receiver is slapping the defender's arms with his left hand and swimming him with his right arm. He does all this before the defender can grab or jam the receiver.

- This is a good slap motion with the receiver's left hand.

CHAPTER 7

Running Pass Routes Versus Bump-and-Run Defenders

Several offenses convert many of their individual pass routes to *fade routes* versus bump-and-run defenders. Defenses look at films and can see this aspect in an offense. Therefore, when they play the bump-and-run, they are anticipating that the receiver will convert his route to a fade. The defender who plays bump-and-run usually takes hundreds of repetitions in practice working on defending this one fade route. Also, the fade route is one of the lowest completion percentage passes an offense has in it's repertoire. However, when faced with an advantageous matchup, it is more than worth the risk.

The receiver who stays on his route when confronted with the bump-and-run defender has a distinct advantage because the defender doesn't practice against all the different routes a receiver can run. In addition, the defender doesn't get to practice against all the different types of releases a good receiver can use in any given play. The defender is always *on his heels* reacting, or guessing at best, as to what the receiver is going to do in any given play.

Receivers should take an outside release to run their routes over 90 percent of the time, even if the route is an inside breaking route. Most receivers will instinctively take an inside release when they are running an inside breaking route. Defenders know this and will usually jump on the receiver's inside hip (assuming the receiver even gets off the line of scrimmage) to get in the *passing lane*. When receivers take an outside release, they usually always know where the defender is, and can set him up before the break is made.

Individual Pass Routes

Quick Hitch

Figure 7-1. Route: Zero versus bump-and-run defenders.

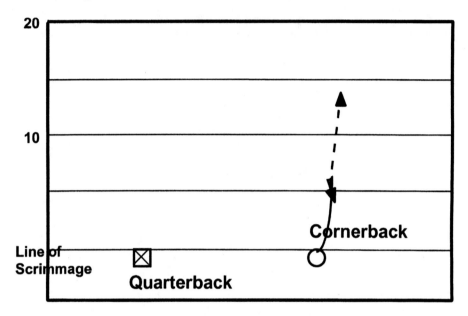

Coaching Points:

- The receiver should close his stance for a lateral movement on the snap of the ball (do *not* lean into the defender).

- The receiver should use a speed release and be sure to knock the defender's hands away.

- The receiver should get an outside release and get even with, *not ahead of*, the defender.

- At six yards the receiver should break down and let the defender's momentum take him downfield past the receiver -- and always turn inside towards the quarterback!

- The receiver should come back *down the stem* hard.

- After making the reception, the receiver should break outside and explode vertically to the goal line.

Note: The receiver may want to convert to the fade route given the right matchup. However, the fade route is usually the lowest percentage pass in an offense. In addition, most offenses do convert many of their routes to fades, so the defense will expect the offense to run the fade. They won't expect the offense to stay on the route.

Quick Speed-Out

Figure 7-2. Route: 1 versus bump-and-run defenders.

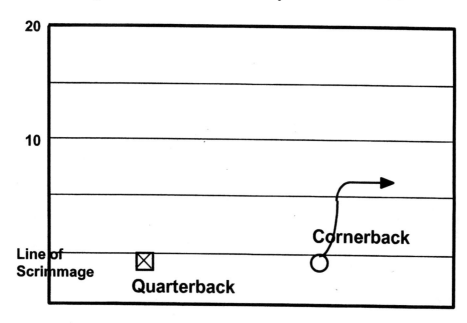

Coaching Points:

- The receiver should close his stance for a lateral movement on the snap of the ball (do *not* lean into the defender).

- The receiver should use a speed release and knock the defender's hands away.

- The receiver should get an outside release and get even with, *not ahead of,* the defender.

- At five yards the receiver should plant his inside foot (*pressure step*) and break hard to the sideline.

- The receiver should let the defender help push him towards the sideline.

- The receiver should accelerate out of his break to the ball.

- After making the reception, the receiver should explode vertically to the goal line.

Quick Slant

Figure 7-3. Route: 2 versus bump-and-run defenders.

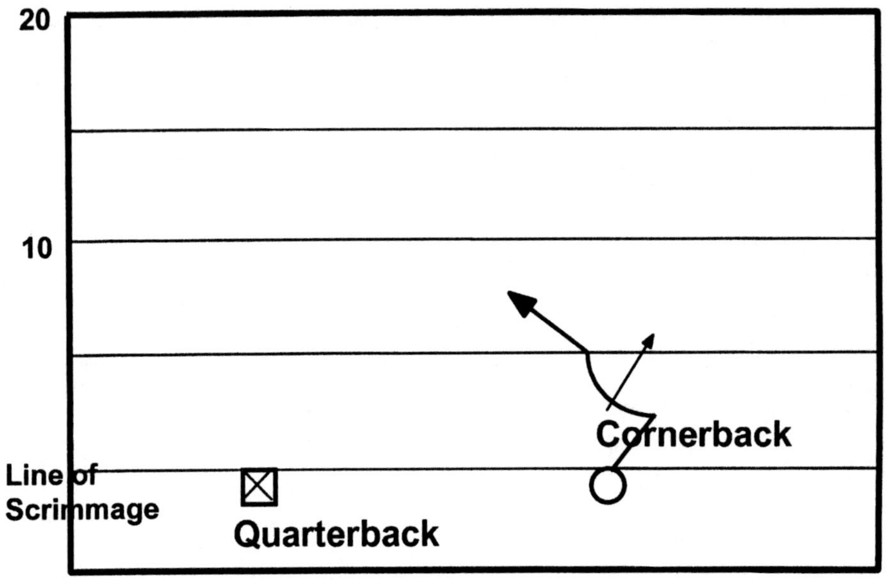

Coaching Points:

- The receiver should close his stance for a lateral movement on the snap of the ball (do *not* lean into the defender).

- The receiver should use an outside speed release and go wider than normal to draw the defender outside with him.

- The receiver should allow the defender to get even with him, or ahead of him, at this point in the route.

- On the receiver's third step, he should hit the breaks and come underneath the defender.

- At five yards the receiver should plant his outside foot (*pressure step*) and break hard to the slant.

- The receiver should accelerate to the ball.

- After making the reception, the receiver should explode vertically to the goal line.

Note: At times, a double-step release will work. The receiver should always get underneath the defender – he should never try to go over the top.

12-Yard Speed-Out

Figure 7-4. Route: 3 versus bump-and-run defenders.

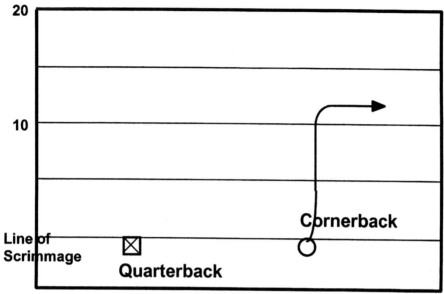

Coaching Points:

- The receiver should close his stance for a lateral movement on the snap of the ball (do *not* lean into the defender).

- The receiver should use a speed release and knock the defender's hands away.

- The receiver should get an outside release and get even with, *not ahead of,* the defender.

- The receiver should get into straight-stem release.

- At 10 yards the receiver should plant his inside foot (*pressure step*) and break hard to the sideline.

- The receiver should let the defender help push him towards the sideline.

- The receiver should accelerate to the ball.

- After making the reception, the receiver should explode vertically to the goal line.

12-Yard Curl

Figure 7-5. Route: 4 versus bump-and-run defenders.

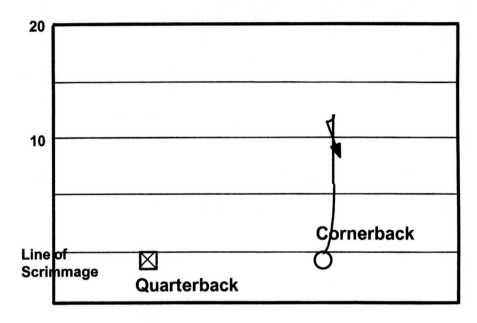

Coaching Points:

- The receiver should close his stance for a lateral movement on the snap of the ball (do *not* lean into the defender).

- The receiver should use a speed release and be sure to knock the defender's hands away.

- The receiver should get an outside release and get even with, *not ahead of*, the defender.

- The receiver should get into straight-stem release.

- At 10 yards the receiver should break down and let the defender's momentum take him downfield past him, and the receiver should always turn inside towards the quarterback! (*top gun* move)

- The receiver should come back *down the stem* hard.

- After making the reception, the receiver should break outside and explode vertically to the goal line.

18-Yard Comeback

Figure 7-6. Route: 5 versus bump-and-run defenders.

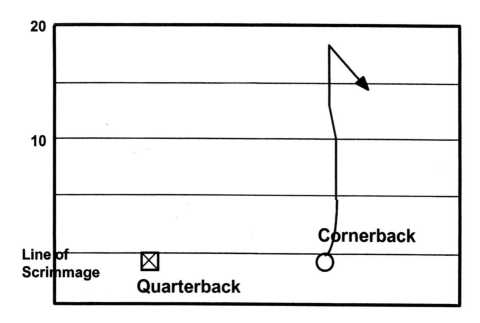

Coaching Points:

- The receiver should close his stance for a lateral movement on the snap of the ball (do *not* lean into the defender).
- The receiver should use a speed release and be sure to knock the defender's hands away.
- The receiver should get an outside release and get even with, or slightly ahead of, the defender.
- At approximately 14 yards the receiver should lean slightly towards the post and look towards the quarterback.
- At 18 yards the receiver should plant his inside foot (*pressure step*) and break hard back to the sideline.
- The receiver should accelerate out of his break and come back to the ball.
- After making the reception, the receiver should explode vertically to the goal line.

16-Yard Dig

Figure 7-7. Route: 6 versus bump-and-run defenders.

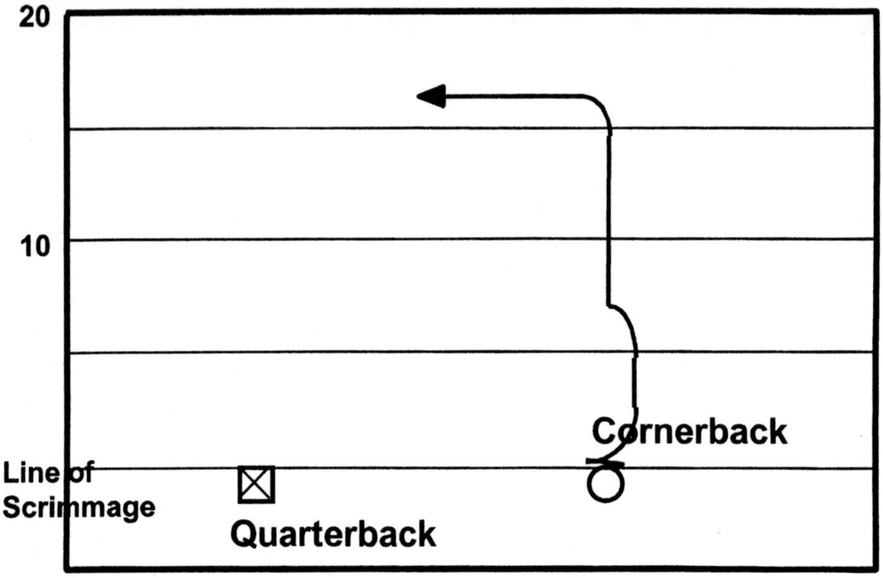

Coaching Points:

- The receiver should close his stance for a lateral movement on the snap of the ball (do *not* lean into the defender).

- The receiver should start with lateral moves; *where you want to go, where you don't want to go, where you want to go.*

- The receiver should get an outside release and get on top of the defender.

- The receiver should push hard into the defender using his hands and body if necessary.

- At approximately eight yards the receiver should plant his inside foot (*pressure step*) and vertically stem the defender.

- At 15 yards the receiver should break to the middle (using a *speed cut* if he is ahead of defender — a *stutter step* if he is even with the defender) and come downhill slightly.

- After making the reception, the receiver should explode vertically to the goal line.

Note: When taking an outside release, the receiver should cut his split down so he ends up where he's supposed to be when the ball is thrown. Also, by cutting his split down, the defense will think he's running an outside breaking route.

16-Yard Dig

Figure 7-8. Route: 6 versus bump-and-run defenders.

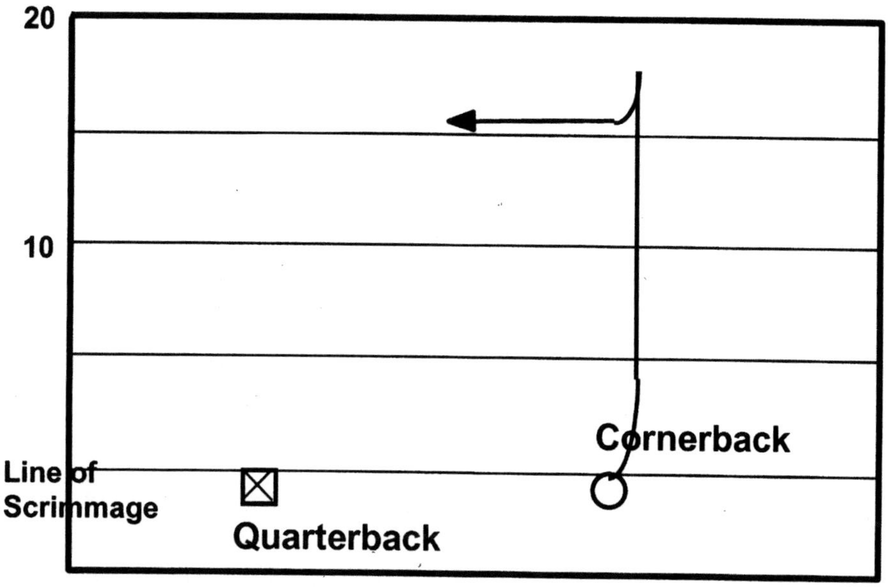

Coaching Points:

- The receiver should close his stance for a lateral movement on the snap of the ball (do *not* lean into the defender).

- The receiver should use a speed release and be sure to knock the defender's hands away.

- The receiver should get an outside release and get even with, *not ahead of*, the defender.

- The receiver should get into a straight stem release.

- At 15 yards the receiver should break down and let the defender's momentum take him downfield past him, and the receiver should always turn inside towards the quarterback! (*top gun* move)

- The receiver should explode towards the middle of the field.

- After making the reception, the receiver should explode vertically to the goal line.

Note: When taking an outside release, the receiver should cut his split down so he ends up where he's supposed to be when the ball is thrown. Also, by cutting his split down, the defense will think he's running an outside breaking route.

16-Yard Dig

Figure 7-9. Route: 6 versus bump-and-run defenders.

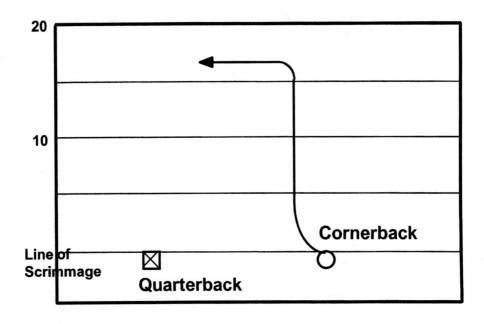

Coaching Points:

- The receiver should close his stance for a lateral movement on the snap of the ball (do *not* lean into the defender).

- The receiver should use a speed release inside.

- On the inside release, the receiver shouldn't get ahead of the defender and not get pushed inside.

- At six to eight yards the receiver should plant his inside foot (*pressure step*) and vertically stem for at least five yards.

- At 15 yards the receiver should lean into the defender and then break away from him.

- The receiver should snap his head to the quarterback and accelerate to the middle of the field.

- After making the reception, the receiver should explode vertically to the goal line.

Note: The receiver should take his normal split because he's using an inside-seam release.

16-Yard Square-In

Figure 7-10. Route: 6 versus bump-and-run defenders.

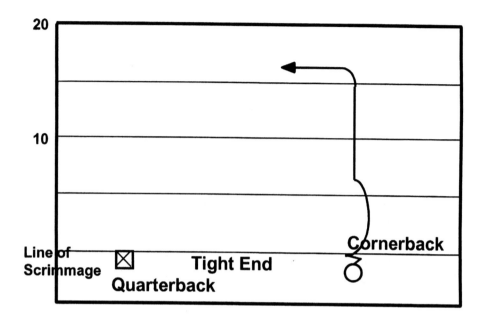

Coaching Points:

- The receiver should close his stance for a lateral movement on the snap of the ball (do *not* lean into the defender).

- The receiver should start with lateral moves; *where you want to go, where you don't want to go, where you want to go.*

- The receiver should get an outside release and try to get over the top of the defender.

- The receiver should push hard into the defender using his arms and body if necessary.

- At approximately eight yards the receiver should plant his inside foot (*pressure step*) and vertically stem the defender.

- At 15 yards the receiver should break to the middle (using a *speed cut* if he's ahead of the defender — a *stutter step* if he is even with the defender) and come downhill slightly.

- After making the reception, the receiver should explode vertically to the goal line.

Note: Remember that the receiver has a route breaking inside of him, so he needs to stay wide. The ball should be in the air before he makes his break to the middle, so be prepared.

16-Yard Square-In

Figure 7-11. Route: 6 versus bump-and-run defenders.

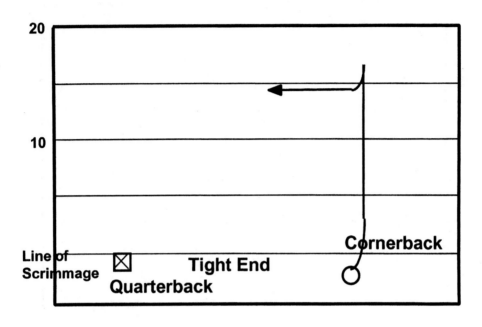

Coaching Points:

- The receiver should close his stance for a lateral movement on the snap of the ball (do *not* lean into the defender).

- The receiver should use a speed release and be sure to knock the defender's hands away.

- The receiver should get an outside release and get even with, *not ahead of,* the defender.

- The receiver should get into a straight-stem release.

- At 15 yards the receiver should break down and let the defender's momentum take him downfield past you, and the receiver should always turn inside towards the quarterback! (*top gun* move)

- The receiver should explode towards the middle of the field.

- After making the reception, the receiver should explode vertically to the goal line.

Note: Remember that the receiver has a route breaking inside of him, so he needs to stay wide. The ball should be in the air before he makes his break to the middle, so be prepared.

12-Yard Post-Corner

Figure 7-12. Route: 7 versus bump-and-run defenders.

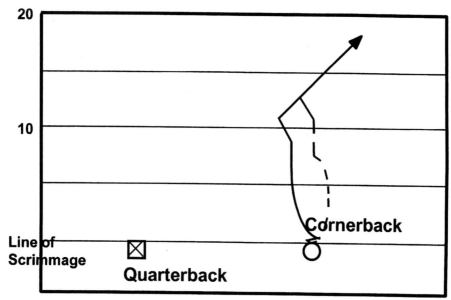

Coaching Points:

- The receiver should close his stance for a lateral movement on the snap of the ball (do *not* lean into the defender).

- The receiver should start with lateral moves; *where you want to go, where you don't want togo, where you want to go.*

- On the inside release, the receiver should get ahead of the defender and not get pushed inside.

- At six to eight yards the receiver should plant his inside foot (*pressure step*) and vertically stem for at least five yards.

- At 10 yards the receiver should make a break to the post route and look to the quarterback.

- At 12 yards the receiver should break towards the flag and accelerate to the ball.

- After making the reception, the receiver should explode vertically to the goal line.

Note: Ideally, the receiver should take the inside release because normally the defender will then jump on his inside hip, allowing him to attain greater separation. However, if the receiver has to go outside, he should go ahead and take it – he should lean into the defender and accelerate to the corner at 12 yards.

12-Yard Post

Figure 7-13. Route: 8 versus bump-and-run defenders.

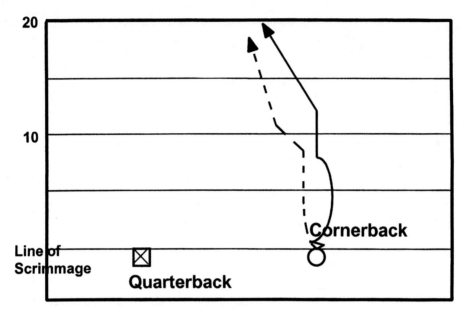

Coaching Points:

- The receiver should close his stance for a lateral movement on the snap of the ball (do *not* lean into the defender).

- The receiver should start with lateral moves; *where you want to go, where you don't want to go, where you want to go.*

- The receiver should get an outside release and get even with the defender, but not get pushed inside.
  - √ The receiver should push hard into the defender using his hands and body. At approximately 8 yards the receiver should plant his inside foot (*pressure step*) and vertically stem the defender.
  - √ At 12 yards the receiver should plant his outside foot (*pressure step*) and accelerate to the post.
  - √ After making the reception, the receiver should explode vertically to the goal line.

Note: Using an inside release, the receiver should push upfield hard, then lean hard into the middle before bursting to the post.

Take-Off

Figure 7-14. Route: Fade versus bump-and-run defenders.

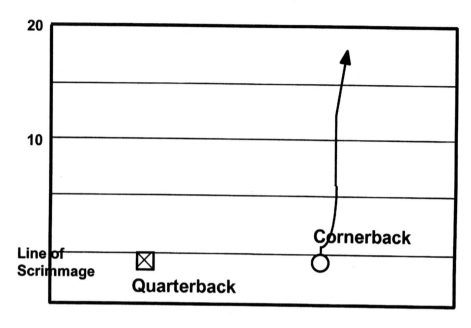

Coaching Points:

- The receiver should close his stance for a lateral movement on the snap of the ball (do *not* lean into the defender).

- The receiver should use his best release (if he has the speed to beat the defender *at that moment* – take it).

- If not, the receiver should get the defender leaning and start with lateral moves; *where you want to go, where you don't want to go, where you want to go.*

- The receiver should get an outside release and go into a straight stem, but not get pushed outside.

- The receiver should lean into the defender as he gets his inside shoulder ahead of the defender's body (using his hands and arms to beat back the defender).

- The receiver should accelerate as he looks back for the ball and fade towards the outside, away from the defender.

Note: This is a timing pass! Realize that the quarterback will throw the ball slightly outside if the defender is running with the receiver to prevent him from getting to the ball.

CHAPTER 8

Advanced Moves for Wide Receivers

The Stick Move

The term *stick* refers to the receiver's ability to make a sudden and distinct change in direction while pushing up the field vertically in a pass route. This sudden change of vertical direction influences the defender's leverage relative to the receiver. The following pictures illustrate how you should teach the *stick move*. The receiver runs downfield on one side of a solid white line. Then, at a predetermined point in the route, the receiver will lean and plant his foot across the line. As this happens, his upper body and feet show a change of direction that is opposite of where the receiver will actually run (Figures 8-1 and 8-2).

Figure 8-1.   **Figure 8-2.**

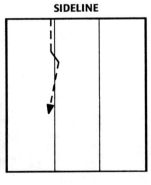

SIDELINE

- The receiver pushes vertically upfield, closing in quickly on the defender.

- The receiver then starts to lean toward the other side of the line.

- He maintains good running form and sets up the move in a subtle manner.

When the receiver plants his foot across the line, he will be in an optimal body position to propel him in the opposite direction back across the line. This snap causes the defender to overreact in a manor that will be detrimental to his coverage capability (Figure 8-3).

Figure 8-3.

- The receiver plants his left foot across the line and has the proper body leverage to propel him back across the line. It is important to remember that this plant foot should be parallel with the line itself. He then accelerates into his route.

When used effectively, this single move can turn a defender around and creates immediate separation. This move is used primarily on the slants, posts, post-corners, and take-off routes, but a version of it is used in the *seam* and *burst* releases.

The Double-Stick Move

The *double-stick move* takes the mastery of the *stick move* before it can even be attempted. It is basically a three-step move and should be executed at near full speed. Once the receiver has used the stick move a few times against an opponent, he can use the double-stick move to really gain separation. A great deal of coordination needs to be learned to do this. This is a great move to use when running post and take-off routes against man-off defenders (Figures 8-4 and 8-5).

Figure 8-4.

Figure 8-5.

SIDELINE

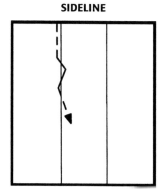

Mid-Stem Moves

Mid-stem moves refer to moves that are initiated at or near the middle of a vertical stem within the pass route. Depending on where in the route the move is made, these moves can create opportunities to get deep on a defender, or create a greater cushion so the receiver has more separation on comeback-type routes.

As a general rule, if a mid-stem move is made further away from the defender (five to seven yards), the move will create separation on routes that break back or away from the defender. If the move is executed closer to the defender (three to five yards) the move will cause the defender to break down or slow down, and allow the receiver to speed by on post or take-off routes.

It should be noted that mid-stem moves do not work well when the receiver does not consistently run his routes at full speed at all times. This means that the receiver cannot run at a pace where he is trying to read what the defender is going to do. The receiver must create *vertical push* on all his routes all the time for mid-stem moves to have any measurable amount of success.

The Stutter Move

The *stutter move* is a good *mid-stem* move to use on routes that break downfield past 15 yards, and should be executed at about 8 to 10 yards from the line of scrimmage. The reason for this is that the defender is expecting a break at that point in the route. When used properly, the defender will automatically react to the move.

The receiver does not want to initiate this move too close to the defender because the defender will be able to get his hands on the receiver if he senses he is going to get beat deep. However, the receiver doesn't want to make the move too far from the defender, because then the defender has no reason to react to it. A good rule of thumb is to use these types of moves when the receiver is within five yards of the defender. Make sure when the receiver comes out of the move he takes at least two more steps before deviating from his stem. This will cause the defender to overreact (Figure 8-6).

The receiver should run full speed at the defender and then start to break down quickly for about three or four steps, and then burst by the defender as he reacts. This same move can be used in deep comeback routes as well.

The receiver will execute the move a little earlier in the route to get the defender to hesitate just a little. The receiver will again attack the defender full speed and then hit the brakes for three or four quick steps – then burst at the defender as if he is going to run by him. The defender has already reacted to one move, so he should really take the bait with the receiver trying to run past him. The defender will naturally try to

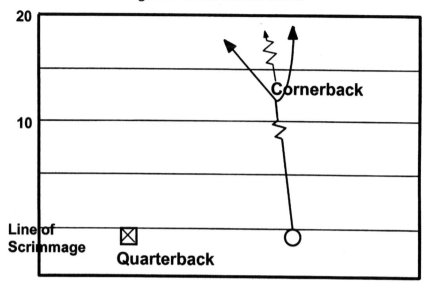

Figure 8-6. The stutter move.

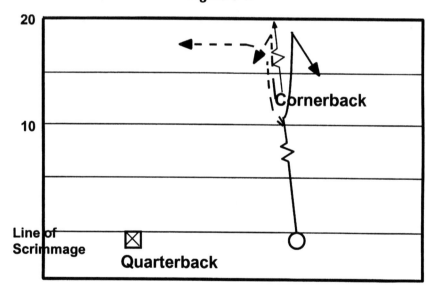

Figure 8-7.

increase his cushion and then give the receiver the necessary space to come back to the ball to make the catch (Figure 8-7).

This is a very good move when play-action is involved versus man-off coverage. The receiver can run deep comebacks, deep curls, or even deep routes breaking across the middle of the field. Again, make sure when the receiver comes out of the move he takes at least two more steps step before deviating from his stem. This will cause the defender to overreact.

The Tiptoe

This is another mid-stem move that really needs a lot of work and practice if it is to be used effectively. This move has the greatest utility when used against very quick, aggressive defenders. If the defender is not a very good athlete, the receiver can just use his speed to beat him.

This *tiptoe move* is good because it gives the illusion of slowing down. However, the reality is that the receiver is not slowing down that much at all. It is much quicker than the stutter move, although the concept is very similar. Unlike the stutter move when the receiver can only really use it in a play-action pass because it takes time and will impede the timing of the play, the tiptoe move can be used in almost any medium for deep breaking routes because it is executed so quickly (Figure 8-8).

Figure 8-8. The tiptoe move.

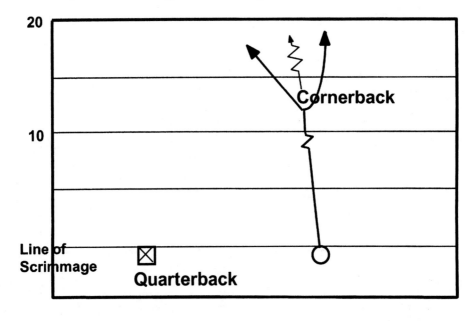

The tiptoe move involves the receiver taking a half-stride in the middle of his stem. What will happen is that at one point both the receiver's feet will be side by side on the ground for a split second, without slowing down a great deal as the receiver usually would if he used the stutter move. The tiptoe move is a good move to use when the receiver needs to get downfield as quickly as possible but still needs to throw a move on the defender. Again, this move really only works against quick and aggressive man-off defenders.

The tiptoe move can also be used a little earlier in the route if the receiver wants to push the defender further downfield. This will get the defender to get deeper in his drop, allowing the receiver greater separation at the break (Figure 8-9).

Figure 8-9.

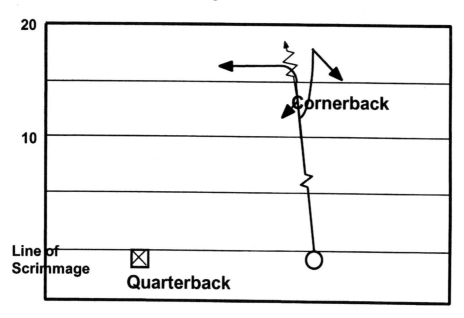

Figure 8-10. The tiptoe move steps.

Step 1

The right foot, in mid-stride, hits the line first (for teaching purposes).

Step 2

The left foot plants even with the right foot (this should be the tiptoe element of the route, and should not tear up any turf).

Step 3

The right foot comes up and continues in stride. This entire move needs to be completed without the receiver standing up in his route.

The Juke Move

This is actually is one of those moves that should be designed into the play. It is used on drag routes. The receiver sprints to a spot over the football, stops, and squares up his shoulders to the quarterback, and then takes off to continue the drag route (Figure 8-11).

Figure 8-11. The juke move.

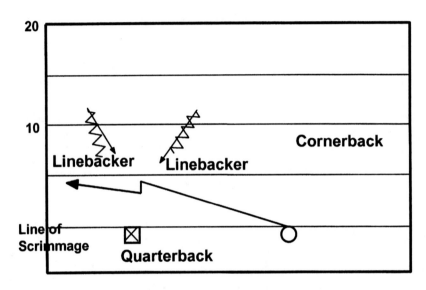

In zone coverage, the *juke move* causes the underneath coverage to attack the spot where the receiver has stopped. They will create a good deal of momentum trying to attack the area. This does two things. First, the dig route or square-in route being run over the top should open up nicely. Second, the linebackers will be attacking an area the receiver will be leaving and will be in a poor position to make a play on him once he receives the ball. In addition, the safeties and corner will be further downfield when the receiver gets the ball, which should increase his *run-after-catch* yards.

The Stair Move

The *stair move* is another move to be used on drag routes. It must be practiced because many times novice receivers can't *feel* when a defender is running with them. The move itself is nothing more than leaning into the defender and almost *shoving* him upfield before continuing the route. This creates immediate separation and allows the receiver to have a clean catch, with no one trying to knock it down. Of course, the move must be just initiated before the quarterback is ready to thrown the pass (Figure 8-12).

Figure 8-12. The stair move.

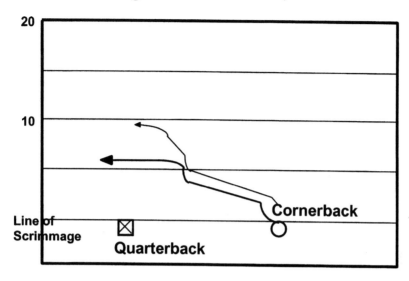

Figure 8-12. The stair move.

The Single-Step Move

The *single-step move* can be used against bump-and-run defenders as well as man-off defenders. The move requires quick and sure footwork. The basic premise is to get the defender to jump on the receiver's move away from where the receiver wants to go. However, this takes great balance and the ability to lean away just before making the break to the open area, away from the defender. This is probably the most common move attempted by novice receivers.

Figure 8-13. The single-step move.

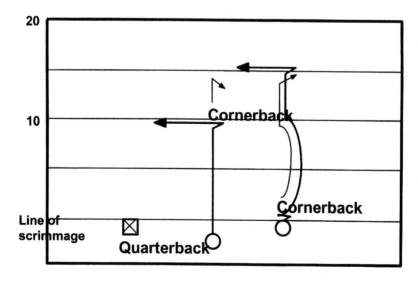

It is also a very effective move when properly utilized as long as the receiver is running the route and executing the move quickly, but not hurried. Again, this should be practiced daily. Many times if this move is not practiced, it fools no one and just allows the defender to better cover the receiver.

The Double-Step Move

The *double-step move* should only be attempted once the single-step move is perfected. It can also be used against bump-and-run defenders as well as man-off defenders. The move requires excellent footwork, and takes hours of practice to perfect. In addition, quick-feet drills should be done long before this type of move is taught.

The premise is to get the defender to jump on the receiver's second move -- away from where he wants to go; *where you want to go, where you don't want to go, where you want to go*. Unfortunately, many receivers do not have the persistence or the technique to master this move.

Figure 8-14. The double-step move.

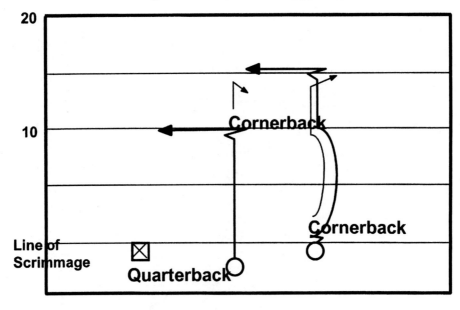

The Slant-Stick Move

The *slant-stick move* is used in the red zone against a man defender, or an aggressive zone defender. The receiver will attack the middle of the defender, lean and *stick* him at approximately two to three yards from the defender. The defender will attempt to get a jump on what he thinks will be the slant route. This will allow the receiver to run the fade route into the end zone (Figure 8-15).

Figure 8-15. The slant-stick move.

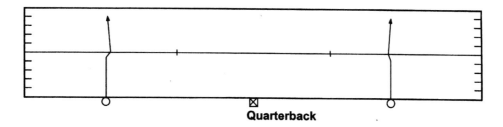

Quarterback

This move will only work when the defender is playing within eight yards of the line of scrimmage, and when he is looking at the receiver at the time of the move. Again, the move should be executed within three yards of the defender. Most of the time, the quarterback will be taking some kind of three-step drop with this type of move.

The Post-Stem Move

This is a great move to use when running square-in and dig routes. It can even be quite effective when running these routes versus cover 2 or quarters-coverage safeties. The receiver takes a vertical release and then breaks to the post at about nine yards. After three to five (at the very most) steps to the post, the receiver breaks vertically once again for another three steps to the outside shoulder of the safety. This will turn the safety to the outside, allowing the receiver to break underneath him and into the open field (Figure 8-16).

Figure 8-16. The post-stem move.

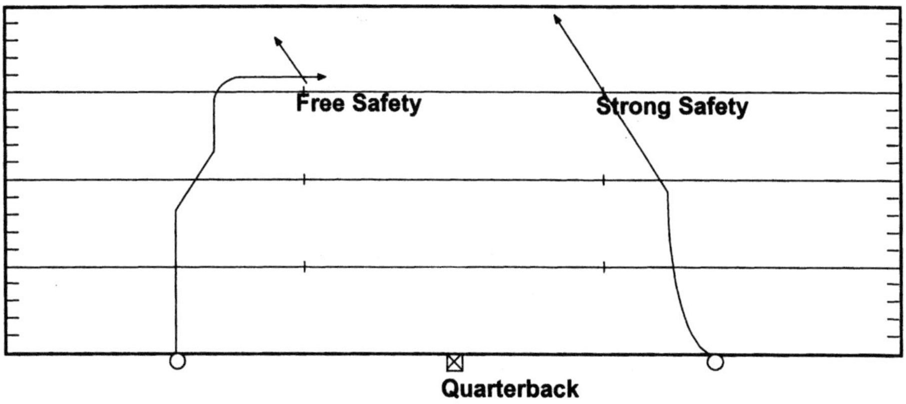

Free Safety   Strong Safety

Quarterback

The other receiver should run some type of post route to occupy the other safety. This will be designed into the pass pattern by the offensive coordinator, and is a common practice with this type of route combination.

CHAPTER 9

Running Counter Routes

Counter routes are routes that show the defender a common base route, and then the receiver will break another way once the defender has *bit* on the route. An example would be an *out-and-up* route. In this route, the receiver will run some type of an out route, either a quick seven-yard out or a 12-yard speed-out, and then break up the sideline on a take-off or streak route. The route is designed to get the defender to jump on the out route, so the receiver can speed past him and get wide open deep down the sideline.

The main problem with these routes is that the receiver running the route can be impatient, and only gives a token fake before breaking upfield. Another problem arises when the receiver makes his initial move too far from the defender, so that even if the defender bit on the move, he is still so far back that he can easily recover to run with the receiver downfield.

One of the best ways to see how a counter route can affect a defender is on a broken play. When the receiver runs his route, he looks back for the ball and he sees the quarterback running for his life. The receiver then instinctively breaks his route and runs in another direction. The defender is unprepared for this and is totally out of position to cover the receiver at this point – he has *sold out* to the original route.

The first thing the receiver has to learn about counter routes is that he must be patient and run the *bait* part of the route just as he would if he were the primary receiver on a timing route. He should attack the defense and snap his head back to the quarterback and get into the route exactly like he normally would. He then needs to break to the counter part of the route, and accelerate out of the break, getting past the defender and the defensive coverage (Figure 9-1).

Figure 9-1. A counter route.

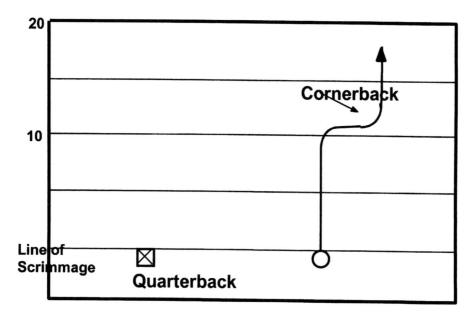

This previous illustration is a good counter route because the receiver makes his break downfield where he normally would. In addition, the receiver breaks hard to the sideline for at least two steps giving the defender time to jump the route and over commit to the sideline. The receiver can then break downfield away from the coverage.

The second thing the receiver needs to realize is that he needs to make his break close enough to the defender so that the defender has to make a break on the route. The following counter route will not work because the defender is so far off the receiver that he has ample time to recover, and run downfield with the receiver (Figure 9-2). In this case, the receiver should have made his initial break to the sideline further downfield (10 yards) so he is closer to the defender. Then the defender would have to jump the route because the receiver breaks right in front of him.

Figure 9-2.

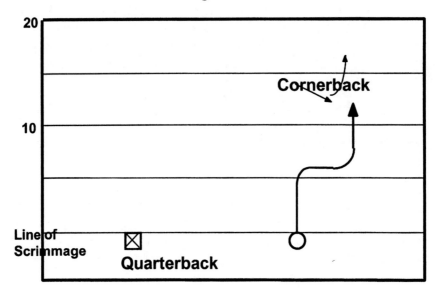

The Quick Hitch and Go

This is a route that should be run when the defender is no deeper than eight yards off the line of scrimmage. This is because the defender has to be in a position where he reacts to the initial break. If the defender is way off the line of scrimmage, a curl and go route would be a more appropriate call. The red zone is a good area to run this in, because the defenders are usually playing the receiver more aggressively (Figure 9-3).

Figure 9-3. The quick hitch and go.

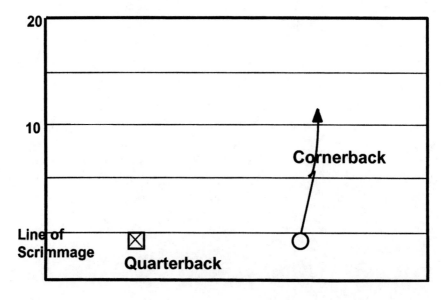

Two points must be made here. First, the receiver must run to a point slightly outside the defender so the receiver can get outside the defender after the fake. The receiver wants to invite the defender to jump the route inside the receiver. Second, the receiver must not spin all the way around (360 degrees) when making the initial move. Instead, the receiver will get to his break point, hesitate while looking back to the quarterback, and then accelerate deep to the open field.

The Quick Out and Up

The *quick out and up* is normally used against an aggressive corner, playing within eight yards of the line of scrimmage. The red zone is a good area to run this route. The receiver will run his normal seven-yard speed-out and maintain eye contact with the quarterback, before breaking up the sideline. If the defender is playing a little deeper, the receiver should make his first break deeper downfield, breaking the defender's cushion. The defender has to at least hesitate before the receiver can make the break towards the goal line (Figure 9-4). It is the play caller's responsibility to know when to call this route. If the defender is playing deeper, the route should break at 12 yards instead of seven yards.

Figure 9-4. The quick out and up.

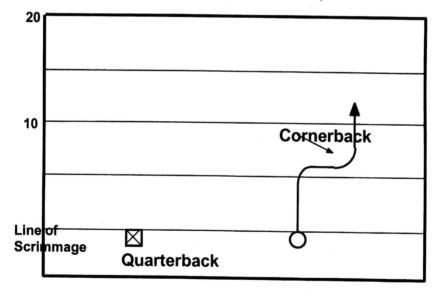

The Slant and Go

The code name for this route in many *West Coast Offenses* is *Sluggo*. This works very well versus quarters coverage when the safety is aggressive against the slant route. The receiver will break to the slant on his third step, and then break up the seam on his sixth step. The receiver is really running this route against a safety even though the corner should bite on the route as well. The quarterback will take a three-step drop, pump fake, and then drop back two more steps before letting the ball go (Figure 9-5).

Figure 9-5. The slant and go.

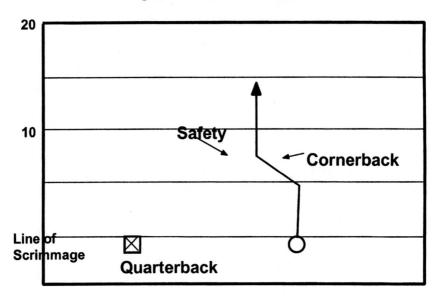

It is important that the receiver run the slant route exactly as he normally would. Receivers tend to run counter routes at less that full speed, but the receiver has to run full speed at all times to make sure he gets enough vertical push to get past the secondary. This route can be run anywhere on the field, except from about the eight-yard line in, where there will most likely not be enough room to make the catch without running out of room in the end zone.

The Out and Up

This route is run a good deal in the NFL. It should be called against defenders who play head-up to inside on the receiver at more than eight yards off the line of scrimmage. This will give the receiver the best opportunity to get by the defender without getting grabbed (Figure 9-6).

The receiver needs to give himself enough room from the sideline so that the catch will be made inbounds. The receiver should make a clean break up the sideline and make sure he does not step out-of-bounds while running downfield.

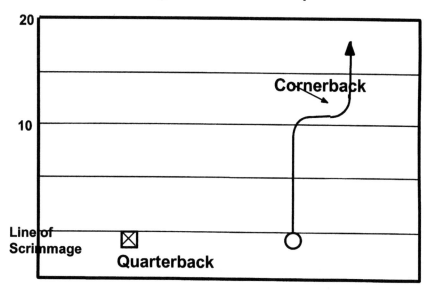

Figure 9-6. The out and up.

The Curl and Go

This is another good route to run against aggressive defenders playing an inside technique more than eight yards off the line of scrimmage. It is the play caller's responsibility to know when to call this route versus perhaps a square-in and go against defenders who are playing an outside technique (Figure 9-7).

Figure 9-7. The curl and go.

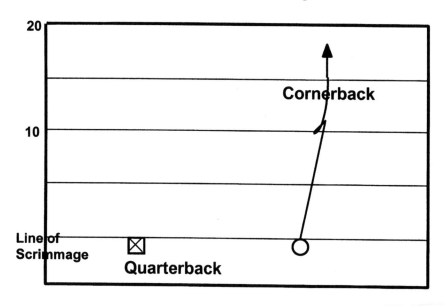

The main reason this route is run against inside-technique defenders is so that the receiver can keep the defender's back towards the quarterback, and still keep the defender in the receiver's peripheral vision. Once again, the receiver does not want to spin around in a 360-degree turn when running this route. Doing this takes too long and gives the defender time to recover and still run downfield. The receiver needs to run full speed, hesitate, look back making eye contact with the quarterback, and then accelerate downfield.

The Square-In and Go

This is a good route to run when the cornerback is playing outside, and the receiver is on the wide side of the field. The receiver will run to the outside shoulder of the corner to push him wider, and then break to the inside at between 10- to 15-yards downfield. The reason for this five-yard break area is that the quarterback doesn't have all day in the pocket, and he needs to get rid of the ball. Although the dig route is usually run a little deeper downfield, the defenders will react to any break in the 10- to 15-yard zone (Figure 9-8).

Figure 9-8. The square-in and go.

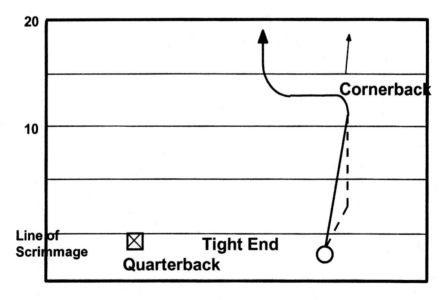

The receiver also has the option of using a burst release to force the corner to gain width, thereby creating more separation from the defender when breaking upfield. Since it is advisable to run this route from the wide side of the field, there will most likely be an inside receiver as well. Usually this number-two receiver will run an outlet route.

The Post Corner

This route was discussed in the base pass route chapter (See Chapter 5). However, it is a counter route with some points to be made it. The best way to run this route is off of a seam release. This gives the receiver the best balance and acceleration when he breaks to the corner. In addition, the receiver should make his initial break or move to the post at about nine-yards downfield. This will give the defender room to jump the post move, but still give the receiver enough room to break underneath the defender to the corner (Figure 9-9).

Figure 9-9. The post corner.

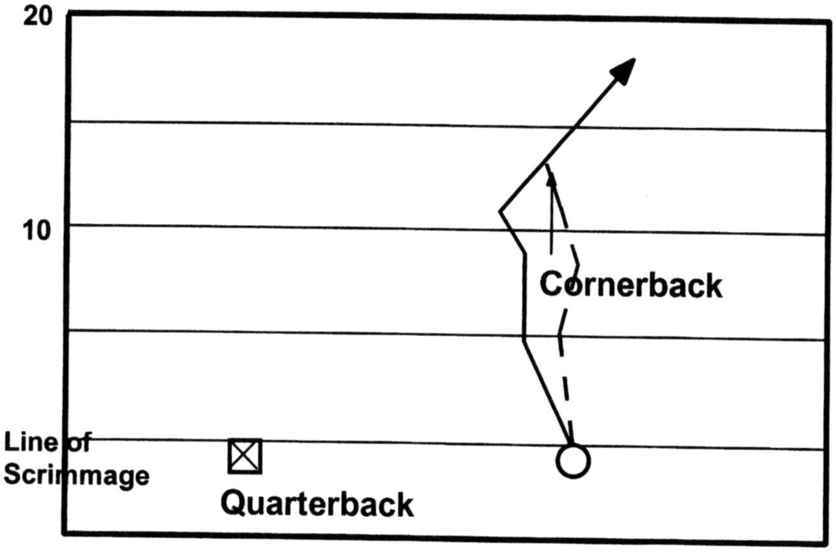

If the defender won't let the receiver inside, and he *walls* the receiver, the receiver can easily go outside the defender, lean to the post, and then accelerate to the corner. It should be noted that as the receiver breaks to the corner, he should accelerate for two strides to make sure he gets the proper separation, before looking back for the ball. It is up to the offensive coordinator to make sure the quarterback has ample protection on these types of routes that require more time to open up downfield.

The Smash

This is an excellent counter route. The smash route simulates the drag route. The defender playing man will usually overcommit to the drag, and as the receiver breaks back to the outside, he will lose the defender. In a zone coverage, when the receiver breaks to the inside, the defender will drop into his zone. As the receiver breaks back outside, he will sit in the zone, make the catch, and then break vertically for the run-after-the-catch yards (Figure 9-10).

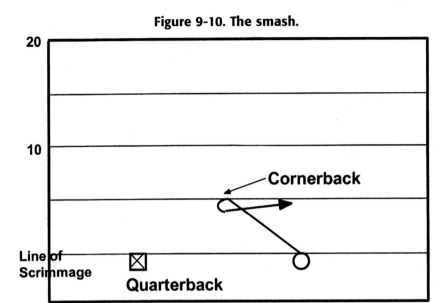

Figure 9-10. The smash.

When the receiver comes out of the drag portion of the route, he needs to stay flat. This creates a better throwing lane because the receiver is separating from the defender. If the receiver gains ground upfield, the defender has the opportunity to make a break on the ball and get the interception.

The V

The *V counter route* is run off of the flat route. The play caller will usually see the defender jumping the flat route, and then call this route. Similar to the *smash* route, the receiver needs to come out of this route somewhat flat when he runs this from the outside or slot positions because he wants to create separation. When running this route out of the backfield, the receiver will take more of steeper angle to get between the linebackers (Figure 9-11).

It's important for the receiver to realize that if he breaks upfield too much when he comes out of the flat route, he will narrow the throwing lane and give the defender a shorter distance to travel to get to the football.

The Fade Back

The *fade back* is an excellent goal line route. The receiver should get across the goal line, look back to the quarterback, and then get in and out of his break as quickly and cleanly as possible. This route should only be called against a bump-and-run defender who does not use a trail technique at the goal line. If the defender does use a trail technique at the goal line, the receiver should run the fade route (Figure 9-12).

Figure 9-11. The V.

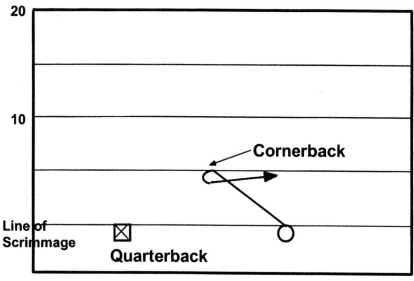

Figure 9-12. The fade back.

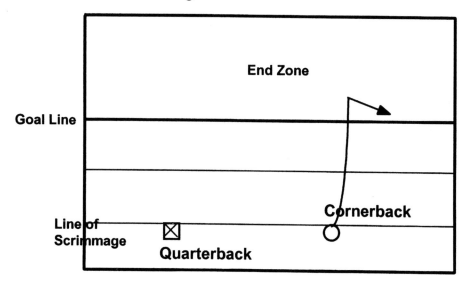

The receiver will use a speed release so that the defender can run beside him. The receiver must run at full speed to get the defender's momentum going in a vertical direction. As the receiver approaches the goal line, he should look back to find the quarterback. Then as the receiver crosses the goal line, he needs to execute the four-step breakdown technique and break hard to the sideline, back for the ball. If the receiver runs less than full speed, the defender will not overreact to the fade route.

CHAPTER 10

Shifting and Going in Motion

Shifting and going in motion can help an offense do several important things. The defense usually has to make some type of adjustment – even if it is a slight adjustment. These techniques help keep the defense at bay.

Shifting is when usually more than one player moves from one set to another before the snap of the ball. The backs can come out of the backfield and line up as receivers, or the tight end can shift from one side of the formation to the other. These shifts change the strength of the formation. *Going in motion* occurs when all eleven players on offense have been in a set position for at least one second, and then only one player moves horizontally behind the line of scrimmage until the snap of the ball.

Shifting

The first important thing to remember about *shifting* is that all of the offensive players need to break the huddle and get to the line of scrimmage as quickly as possible. Second, the first *set* of the players (where they start before they shift) needs to appear from the defense's perspective to be the position the offense will be in when the ball is finally snapped. If an offensive player in an initial set position gives the impression that he is about to shift, the defense can sense this and then be ready for the shift. The shift should either slightly surprise the defense, or at least have them *on their heels* before the snap of the ball. Third, all the players that shifted must be in a set position for at least one second before the ball is snapped, or before another offensive player goes in motion.

The following diagram illustrates a shift (Figure 10-1). The tight end changes sides, thereby changing the strength of the formation. The backs shift from the backfield to *wing* positions. The defense first sees a somewhat normal, two-back formation that changes to an *empty* look – hopefully surprising them.

Figure 10-1. Shifting.

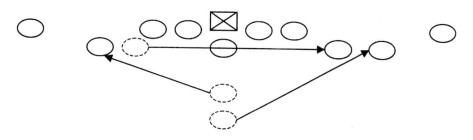

Going in Motion

A few important points need to be mentioned here about *going in motion*. First, the offense needs to get to the line of scrimmage quickly. Second, the receiver needs to make sure that all the shifting has been completed and that everyone is set for at least one second *before* the motioning back or receiver goes in motion. A simple rule to remember is that if the receiver is in motion and sees one of his teammates move, the receiver should come to a complete stop for at least one second before continuing in his motion. Third, the receiver should move quickly to the area he will be moving to before that snap of the ball, and then slow down a bit, and turn his shoulders so they are parallel with the line of scrimmage before the snap of the ball. The reason for this is simple: when the receiver's shoulders are parallel with the line of scrimmage, he can then move inside, vertically, or outside at the snap of the ball. If the receiver has his shoulders perpendicular to the line of scrimmage at the snap of the ball, it is more difficult for him to have the same three-way go at the snap of the ball (Figures 10-2 through 10-4).

Figure 10-2. Going in motion.

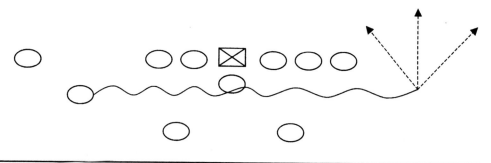

Figure 10-3.

- The receiver is motioning across the formation watching how the defense reacts.

- The receiver moves quickly to the area he is going to be in when the ball is snapped.

Figure 10-4.

- The receiver squares up his shoulders so they are parallel to the line of scrimmage just before the ball is snapped.

- The receiver can then break to the inside, vertically, or to the outside as soon as the ball is snapped.

Exceptions to these rules are as follows. If the receiver is going to run some kind of *rub* route, it is sometimes beneficial to get out of the backfield as quickly as possible, even if that momentum takes him slightly outside with no real threat of breaking back against the grain to run a route to the inside of the field (Figure 10-5).

Figure 10-5.

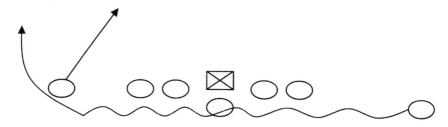

The receiver should also know what the defense is doing to adjust to this movement. If a man is running with the motioning player, it is some type of man coverage. If the defense *bumps* or shifts slightly, it is usually some type of zone coverage.

Shifting and going in motion should be practiced every week, but kept isolated from practicing plays. It is wasting valuable practice time learning how to shift and go in motion when a play or series of plays is being installed. You should only take about 5 to 10 minutes at the beginning of the practice week to practicing shifting and going in motion.

Figure 10-6.

CHAPTER 11

Wide Receiver Blocking

A wide receiver that can block is extremely valuable to an offense. Not many runs gain a lot of yards without a block from the receiver. The wide receiver should have a basic understanding of his offensive running game. He should know which hole the ball is being run through as well as what the chances are for a cut-back run. The receiver should also understand the timing of the run. That is to say, when will the ballcarrier be in a position to cut off of the receiver's block. The receiver should also be familiar with how the running back will set up the receiver's downfield block. The running back should be able to accelerate past the receiver's block, or dip inside or outside to get the defender to commit one way or the other, enabling the receiver to *take the defender where he wants to go.*

Four basic blocks from the wide receiver will be discussed in this chapter. These four blocks begin with technique and timing, and should always be practiced on a daily basis for them to become effective on game day. The four blocks are: the stalk, the cut, the convoy, and the crack block.

The Stalk Block

The *stalk block* is the cornerstone of blocking to the wide receiver. This block takes timing and technique – not brute strength. Proper instruction can make a wide receiver into a competent stalk blocker.

Figure 11-1.

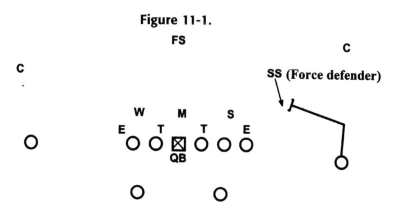

It is important that the receiver know where the ball is being run to -- he must know where to block the defender. If the receiver has the *force defender*, he may be assigned to block a safety coming up to make the tackle (Figures 11-1 and 11-2).

Figure 11-2.

If the receiver's only responsibility is to block the man covering him (usually the cornerback), he must burst off the line of scrimmage to get the defender on his heels before he can recover and come up to attempt to make a tackle (Figure 11-3).

Figure 11-3.

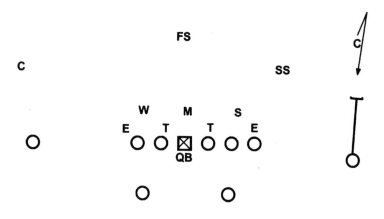

The receiver will attack the man he is going to stalk block. He will break down within three to five yards before making contact. If the receiver runs with too much momentum towards the defender, the receiver will have a tendency to lunge at the defender, and miss the block completely. The receiver should sprint to an area in front of the defender, break down a bit, and then make the block (Figure 11-4).

Figure 11-4.

- The receiver does a good job breaking down in front of the defender. He will then engage the defender and block him in the appropriate direction.

The positioning and hand placement of the receiver will very much resemble an offensive lineman in a pass-blocking drill. The difference being that the receiver will not give up ground to the defender, but rather stop the defender's path to the ballcarrier, or any area that the defender wants to go to (Figure 11-5).

Figure 11-5.

- The receiver will engage the defender with his arms extended to the chest area of the defender. The receiver should keep his hands inside the defender's shoulders and should not grab outside that area.

If the receiver needs to keep the defender from heading to the tackle box, the receiver will swing his rear to the direction he is preventing the defender from going to, or wall off the defender, after the initial contact has been made. This type of blocking is most often needed when the ballcarrier is running between the tackles (Figure 11-6).

Figure 11-6.

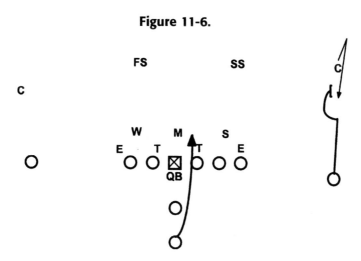

If the ballcarrier is running a sweep, toss, or pitch to the outside, the receiver will first make contact, then push the defender wherever the defender first attempts to go. For example, many times a running back will set the receiver's block up by running to the inside of the receiver. The defender sees this and reacts by trying to run to the receiver's inside. As the defender starts to the inside, the receiver will swing his rear to the outside and, with the defenders momentum, take him to the inside. The running back will then bounce the play to the outside, which is free of defenders (Figure 11-7).

Figure 11-7.

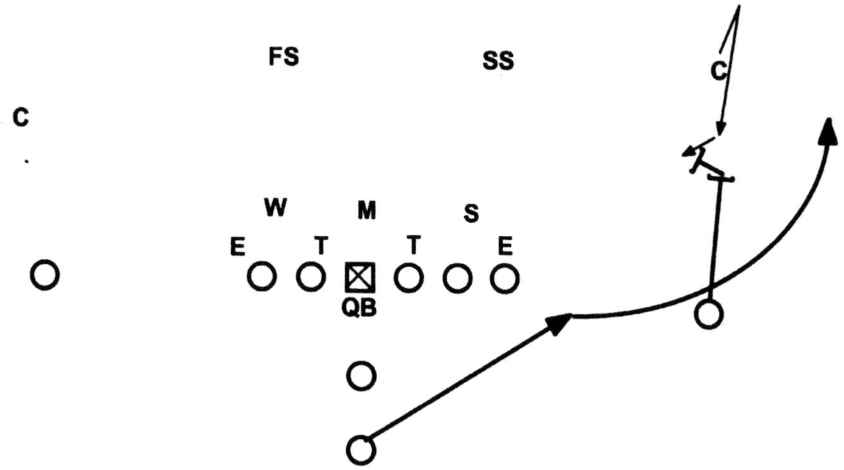

The Cut Block

The *cut block* can be a very effective block if it is timed properly. It is also a great way to still make a block if the receiver is stalking the defender, but starts to lose him. The cut block can also be used to psychologically impair the defender by getting him to worry more about what the receiver will try to do, rather than trying to get to the ballcarrier.

The receiver must wait until the last split second before he goes to cut the defender – timing is everything. The receiver will still attack the defender as he would if he were stalking him. Once he gets to within a couple of yards of the defender, the receiver can either engage in the stalk block, or go right for the cut block.

To throw a cut block, the receiver will aim for a point above the defender's knee. At no time will the receiver attack the defenders' knee, because this could severely injure the player – and even end his career. If the receiver aims for a point below the defenders knee, the defender can easily push the receiver into the ground, and step over him (Figure 11-8).

Figure 11-8.

• The receiver has made contact with the defender. Hopefully, this will bring the defender to the ground if executed properly.

As the receiver attacks the defender's thigh area, he wants to make contact between the back of his own shoulder and upper back, and the defender's thigh. At the same time, the receiver will throw his *onside* arm forward, and reach out over his own head. When the receiver makes contact, he should begin to roll into the defender, and continue to do so until the whistle blows.

Once the receiver makes contact with the ground, he will continue to roll into the defender and pull his knees up into his chest area. As he rolls into the defender, his knees will act as another barrier to the ballcarrier if the defender is not on the ground (Figure 11-9).

Ideally, the initial contact will cut the defender's legs out from under him, knocking him to the ground. Defensive backs are excellent athletes though, and unless the receiver continues to roll into the defender, the defender will pop back up and still have an opportunity to make a play.

Figure 11-9.

• After the initial contact has been made, the receiver should continue to roll into the defender. The knees will stay tucked into the chest throughout the block. If the legs extended at all, the referee could call tripping.

The receiver should not attempt to trip the defender with a leg whip. This is an easy call for the referee to make, and may cost the offense 15 yards. Instead, when the receiver keeps rolling into the defender with his knees pulled up near his chest, the defender will have a difficult time getting rid of the block.

The Convoy Block

The *convoy block* is a simple block, but very necessary. This block is used when the ball is going to the other side of the field. Assuming some type of zone secondary, the receiver will take off towards the middle of the field and head for the safety on the far side of the field. If any defender crosses the receiver's face as he runs at this 40-degree angle across the field, the receiver will block him right away — a cut block is appropriate as long as the receiver gets up right away and makes sure that defender does not get near the play (Figure 11-10).

Figure 11-10.

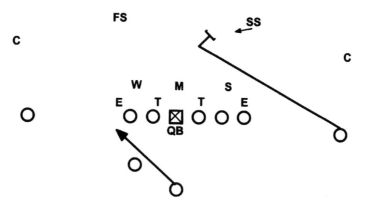

When the receiver takes off on his path to the far safety, he needs to watch what the safeties are doing, as well as being able use his peripheral vision to sense where the play is going. Many times the running back will cut back and run towards the middle of the field. The receiver will be in a great position to make a key block here and spring the back for a big gain (Figure 11-11).

Figure 11-11.

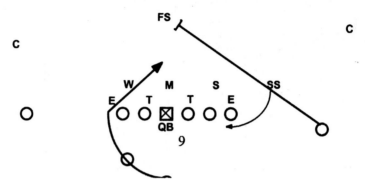

The Crack Block

The *crack block* is a block on a linebacker or a defensive end that doesn't know it is coming. The receiver's job is to knock the defender totally out of the play. The running back will be taking the ball to the outside (Figure 11-12).

Figure 11-12.

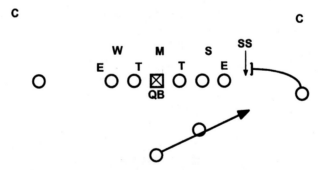

The key with this block is to make solid contact with the target. The receiver's head should be on the frontside of the defender (if it isn't, the receiver could be called for *clipping*), and the receiver must make sure his block is *above the waist* (if it isn't, he will be called for *blocking below the waist*). It is also important that the receiver make good, solid contact without lunging. Usually, when a blocker lunges, he will put is head down and may miss the target completely (Figure 11-13).

Figure 11-13.

• The receiver's head must be in front of the man being blocked so that he will not be called for *blocking in the back*. In addition, the crack block must be executed *above the waist* of the defender. At no time will the receiver block the man *below the waist*.

The cornerback should make a *crack* call as the receiver approaches his target. This does not always happen, and if it does, sometimes the target is so intent on getting to the ballcarrier, he disregards the call all together. If the target beats the receiver across the line of scrimmage, the receiver should come off the block rather than hit the defender in the back.

Not that many offensive plays include the receiver getting to crack block. However, when the crack block is executed well, the play usually gains good yardage, and the defender surprisingly enough gains respect for the receiver.

The Run Off

The *run off* is used when the defender is in bump-and-run coverage. In most cases, it doesn't matter where the ball is going, the receiver will just occupy his man by *running him off downfield* (Figure 11-14). However, it is important to remember that the defender may peek back into the backfield, realize the play is a run, and then come off the receiver and try to make the tackle. The receiver needs to be cognizant of this, and be ready to break down and block the defender. If the ballcarrier is far from the defender, the stalk block is appropriate. However, if the ballcarrier is close to the defender, the receiver can cut the defender, as long as the receiver doesn't cut him from behind (this is called a *chop block* and is illegal).

The receiver should always be blocking someone on every run play, regardless of where the run is going. This will keep the defender thinking about what the receiver is doing on every play. Receivers should mentally condition themselves to never take a play off. This mindset is more mental that physical, and will usually help the offense make some big plays because the receiver took care of his responsibility and made a quality block.

Figure 11-14.

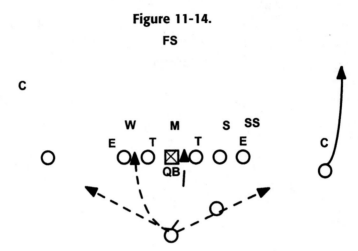

CHAPTER 12

Contingency Plans for Wide Receivers

Many times during a football game a quarterback will drop back, and for one reason of another, the protection breaks down, or he can't find anyone open. In these cases, the quarterback has several choices. First, he can throw the ball away, which stops the clock. At certain times this is the appropriate decision. Second, he can take the sack, which keeps the clock running. Other times this is the correct choice. Third, the quarterback can go to a contingency plan and make a play downfield. The receiver will run his route, make his break, and create separation from the defender. The receiver realizes that the quarterback is taking off laterally. This is when the receiver has to make the appropriate adjustment – the contingency plan.

The Contingency Plan

When a pass play breaks down, the receivers should run to specific areas on the field to form a triangle of opportunity for the quarterback. The receivers should make the appropriate adjustments to get open. The widest receiver to the side the quarterback is moving to should take the deep area to that side. The inside receiver should slide at a depth between the line of scrimmage and the deepest receiver, and the receiver furthest from the quarterback should slide horizontally and slightly upfield. As the quarterback rolls to one side or the other, he can keep the ball or throw to one of the receivers (Figures 12-1 and 12-2).

Figure 12-1.

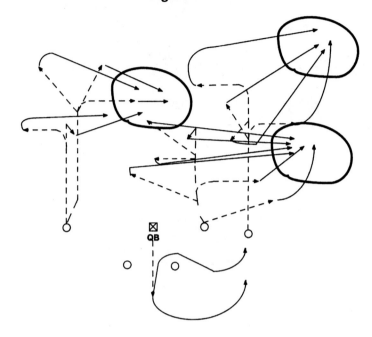

Figure 12-2.

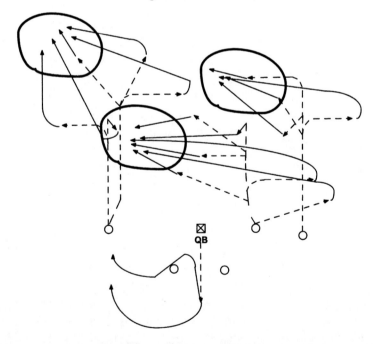

If running backs are involved in the play, they will also go to the appropriate open area. This type of contingency plan can create big plays. However, this type of plan should be practiced for it to become *second nature* for the players.

The Quick-Passing Game Contingency Plan

In the quick-passing game, the quarterback has to lose ground and then slide horizontally. The receiver's basic rules are the same. The widest receiver to the side the quarterback is moving to should take the deep area to that side. The inside receiver should slide at a depth between the line of scrimmage and the deepest receiver, and the receiver furthest from the quarterback should slide horizontally and slightly upfield (Figures 12-3 and 12-4).

Figure 12-3.

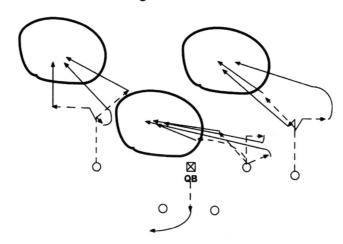

Figure 12-4.

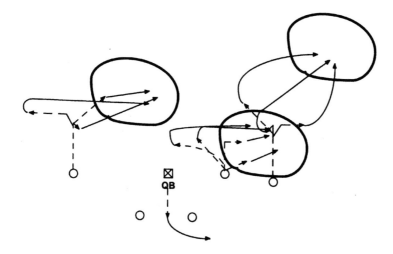

ABOUT THE AUTHOR

Ron Jenkins is the quarterbacks/receiver coach and passing game coordinator at El Camino College, a community college located in Torrance, California. In addition to his present position, which he has held since 1998, Ron also teaches mathematics at a private high school in Torrance, CA.

Ron grew up in Santa Rosa, California, where he was a record-setting track performer in high school. He then played football for two years at Santa Rosa Junior College, before accepting a football scholarship in 1982 to play wide receiver at Colorado State University. Following his senior season at CSU, Ron signed with the Dallas Cowboys and spent an injury-plagued 1984 season with the Cowboys as a wide receiver. The following year he was released off the injured list. He then returned to Colorado State, where he completed his bachelor's degree in psychology in 1985. Subsequently, he moved to Los Angeles to attend graduate school and earned a masters degree in marriage, family, and child counseling from California State University. He is also working on a second masters degree in administration.

Ron began his coaching career in 1994 at Santa Monica Junior College (CA), where he spent two years as the wide receivers and quarterbacks coach. In 1996, he was hired as the offensive coordinator and quarterbacks coach at Los Angeles Harbor College. During his tenure on the Seahawks' staff, LAHC scored more points than any other football team in school history and set most of the school's offensive records.

Ron is a prolific writer who has authored three other books—*101 West Coast Offense Plays, Quarterback Play: Fundamentals and Techniques*, and *Coaching the Multiple West Coast Offense*—in addition to a number of articles for various coaching magazines and professional journals. He has been featured on four best-selling videos on the Multiple West Coast Offense. He is a much sought-after clinician who has addressed coaching clinics across the country. Single, he currently resides in Torrance, California. He may be contacted at ronnyball@aol.com.